Customary Law in Papua New Guinea

A Melanesian View

Customary Law in Papua New Guinea

A Melanesian View

Edited by

RICHARD SCAGLION

Law Reform Commission of Papua New Guinea
Monograph No. 2

ISBN 0 7247 0746 8

Printed at the Government Printing Office, Papua New Guinea and published by the Law Reform Commission of Papua New Guinea. Cover illustration and frontispiece courtesy of Richard Scaglion.

For the people of Papua New Guinea.

Map of Papua New Guinea showing districts from which the researchers collected material.

1. Nuku, West Sepik
2. Maprik, East Sepik
3. Wewak, East Sepik
4. Bogia, Madang
5. Madang, Madang
6. Finschhafen, Morobe
7. Lorengau, Manus
8. Taskul, New Ireland
9. Namatanai, New Ireland
10. Talasea, West New Britain
11. Rabaul, East New Britain
12. Buin, North Solomons
13. Laiagam, Enga
14. Kandep, Enga
15. Mt. Hagen, Western Highlands
16. Pangia, Southern Highlands
17. Chuave, Simbu
18. Henganofi, Eastern Highlands
19. Daru, Western
20. Vailala, Gulf
21. Kupiano, Central
22. Losuia, Milne Bay
23. Tufi, Northern
24. Northern

CONTENTS

INTRODUCTION

Richard Scaglion

Virtually all of the published information on customary law in Papua New Guinea involves interpretations of Melanesian law by non-Nationals. This volume represents an alternative approach: Melanesians analyzing and restating the customary law practices of their own societies. Through this approach we hope to present, insofar as possible, a unified and "indigeneous" categorization and presentation of customary law rather than a classification based on a legalistic or academic western framework.

The papers in this collection represent summaries of principles of customary law written by University of Papua New Guinea student researchers who worked in their home areas over their long vacations in either 1979-80 or 1980-81. They are meant to describe the emic or "insiders' " view of customary law as seen through the eyes of members of their respective societies. The data on which the papers are based include extended case studies, interviews and written records. The research was done for the Customary Law Development Project of the Law Reform Commission of Papua New Guinea.

The Customary Law Development Project was designed to provide the basis for developing a Papua New Guinean legal system based on Papua New Guinea values, customs, beliefs, perceptions and institutions. It was expected to gather customary law materials with a view to developing such materials along national policy lines and integrating any underlying principles discovered into a self-reliant and uniquely Melanesian national legal system.

The project began in June 1979. The first several months were spent in organizing project activities. Initially, extensive bibliographical research was conducted which resulted in the identification of hundreds of sources on customary law in Papua New Guinea. These references are being catalogued according to subject matter and geographical area, and eventually will be published by the Law Reform Commission as a Bibliography of Customary Law in Papua New Guinea.

Examination of these bibliographic sources underlined the need for more detailed and more complete research on the subject of customary law in specific Papua New Guinea societies. Most of the articles on customary law in Papua New Guinea either deal with customary law in general, or mention in passing the customary law or customary conflict cases in particular societies when dealing with other subjects. Also, there was a geographical bias, with several areas of the country overrepresented in these studies. Several alternative strategies for gathering primary data were investigated; including the use of magistrates, foreign anthropologists, student researchers, etc. It was decided that major primary data on a broad representative sample of customary legal systems in PNG would best be gathered by University students working in their home areas over their long study break.

Methodology

In order to develop a comparative methodology for this research, pilot studies were conducted in the Maprik area of the East Sepik Province, familiar to the Project Director from previous customary law research. The specific purpose of these pilot studies was to investigate the practicality of using Village Court records for primary data collection, to refine data gathering instruments, and to establish an overall approach.

Village Court records proved to be rather unreliable and scanty and were used mainly for corroborative data. Village Courts themselves proved to be an interesting forum for customary law applications, however, and many of the student researchers gathered data on Village Court hearings. These data were best obtained through questioning Village Court magistrates about how they applied customary law in particular cases. That is, cases had to be observed or investigated: formal records were inadequate for our purposes. A summary paper analyzing Village Court records from the pilot area and indicating shortcomings of such records for purposes of recording customary law appeared in the *Melanesian Law Journal* (Scaglion 1979).

Investigation of the customary law of the Abelam people in this area revealed relatively few generally agreed upon substantive rules. Their customary legal system appeared to be less of a system of application of formal legal rules to a given fact situation and more a flexible and changing system of ensuring an equitable solution through compromise. Thus it was decided that the overall data-collection strategy should focus on the collection of original conflict case studies, from which substantive principles of customary law in particular societies could be extracted. These cases could then also be analyzed as a homogeneous data base to investigate possibilities for cross-cultural national unification of customary law. A summary of Abelam customary law, together with implications for legal planning in Papua New Guinea appears in Scaglion (1981).

Once the general strategy of data collection through the case method had been established, it remained to develop schedules for recording cases specially designed for this research. These schedules were based upon ones used by the Project Director in his 1974-1976 research (Scaglion 1976). Each case contained, as a minimum, the following information: (a) date and time of occurrence of significant events concerning the case; (b) sources of information concerning the case; (c) pertinent biographical information on the actors including bystanders and those who may have precipitated the conflict but may not have been present; (d) the history of any previous conflict between the individuals involved; (e) the history of this particular conflict including the disposition made by any remedy agents previously used; (f) the reasons for the conflict and each actor's perceptions of the facts they considered to be important; (g) the disposition made by various remedy agents and the reasons given for their decisions; (h) any evidence for underlying issues; (i) evidence concerning the consequences of the case including the effects on the relationships between the parties involved and as a possible precedent for future cases; and (j) differences in decisions and/or procedures for similar conflicts in the past.

This information was organized into several categories which formed the basis for data organization case forms on which all cases gathered by the researchers were recorded. These categories included: 1) researcher, 2) village, 3) case number, 4) date, 5) informants, 6) summary of facts, 7) conflict history, 8) relationship between parties, 9) dispositions of remedy agents and reasons for disposition/decision, 10) principles of customary law involved/discussed, and 11) addenda. Cases of various types were to be collected including memory cases of conflicts occurring in the past (useful for establishing an historical baseline), hypothetical cases (where imaginary situations are described by researchers and customary law discussed by informants), and actual conflict cases occuring in the villages when researchers were present. The collection of data according to a formal schedule assured that no particular type of information would be inadvertently forgotten. It allowed for an adequate description of the specifics of each case, yet provided a general framework for the classification and statistical analysis of cases which is presently underway.

Nearly 600 extended case studies were collected in this manner. These are being coded according to such variables as type of case, geographical area, remedy agents used and decision reached. A computer retrieval system has been written to allow legal researchers to scan the types of cases they are interested in and receive a print-out of summary information about the cases together with case numbers of individual cases. These case identification numbers can then be used to retrieve the original cases from files for further detailed study. In this way, a basic corpus of customary law cases has been created for use in developing the underlying law of Papua New Guinea in accordance with Law Reform Commission Report No.7 (1977). Case numbers used by researchers in their reports refer to these extended case identification numbers.

Researchers attended a series of seminars designed to familiarize them with the specific aims of the project and with the data collection methodology. For a period of about 12 weeks, either during the long University vacation in 1979-1980 or 1980-1981, students gathered data. In many cases, researchers were either supervised in the field or were provided with feedback on their progress by either the Project Director or Project Officer. Upon return from the field, researchers attended another seminar on writing their final reports, which were to be in the form of restatements of customary law in their areas. They were not given any standard model or format for the organization of these reports: it was thought that customary law should not be forced into unnatural categories, particularly not the categories of western jurisprudence. Thus each researcher was free to design his own format, which was to reflect indigeneous perceptions of customary law.

The lack of a standardized format, although intentional, has made the editing of these reports a difficult task, particularly since English is a second language for virtually all of the researchers. Consequently substantial editing including some rewriting and reorganization of reports was necessary to present this report in standardized English as a coherent whole. In editing I have tried not to change the sense of passages or distort customary legal structures reported by the researchers. In some cases which could not be checked, ambiguities were left in reports. While a certain amount of distortion is inevitable, I have attempted to let the researchers speak for themselves and have only clarified their English. In any case, the original unedited reports remain in the Law Reform Commission in case of uncertainty of interpretation.

The Sample of Societies

It was intended to have at least one researcher in every Province. We wanted to have as broad or representative a sample of societies as possible; consequently we selected some fieldsites close to towns, some in rather remote areas, etc. There is a slight bias towards "acculturated" areas in the sample, reflecting the fact that relatively unacculturated areas do not have University Students in great numbers if at all. This should offset the bias of anthropological

Table 1

CHAPTER	RESEARCHER	AREA	PROVINCE	DEPARTMENT	NUMBER OF CASES COLLECTED
1	Matthew Wramainiken	Nuku	West Sepik	Arts	6
2	Raymond Kamanabi	Maprik	East Sepik	Soc/Anthro	21
3	Tarcissius Muganaua	Wewak	East Sepik	Soc/Anthro	9
4	James Gissua	Bogia	Madang	Arts	9
5	Sanol Malaga	Madang	Madang	Law	9
6	Jamoa Morriss	Finschhafen	Morobe	Law	46
7	Fraser Pitpit	Lorengau	Manus	Law	7
8	Soiat Williams	Taskul	New Ireland	Education	8
9	Sios Naibucka	Namatanai	New Ireland	Law	6
10	Cosmos Token Kaue	Talasea	West New Britain	Law	12
11	Jennifer Totabu	Rabaul	East New Britain	Arts	10
12	Regis Stella	Buin	North Solomons	Arts	11
13	David Lambu	Laiagam	Enga	Law	43
14	James Liu Fox	Kandep	Enga	Law	30
15	Veronica Amnol	Mt. Hagen	Western Highlands	Law	18
16	Robert Paia	Pangia	Southern Highlands	Soc/Anthro	7
17	Franklin Artihulawa	Chuave	Simbu	Law	16
18	Mao Rob Atiyafa	Henganofi	Eastern Highlands	Arts	16
19	Mapesa Dume	Daru	Western	Arts	5
20	Hauka Hulape	Vailala	Gulf	Law	45
21	Wari Iamo	Kupiano	Central	Soc/Anthro	51
22	Danniel Mark	Losuia	Milne Bay	Law	—
23	Marcel Dixon Mes	Tufi	Northern	Arts	—
24	Nicodemus Araho	Popondetta	Northern	Arts	14
	Other Researchers				
	Herowa Agiwa	Koroba	Southern Highlands	Soc/Anthro	—
	Aita Ivarato	Okapa	Eastern Highlands	Education	10
	Aria Hailaeavila	Vailala	Gulf	Soc/Anthro	46
	Xystus Kinala	Pomio	East New Britain	Arts	20
	Graham Smith Sem	Tufi	Northern	Arts	30
	Kauzi Yandabing	Morobe	Morobe	Arts	36
					541

literature towards less acculturated areas. We also selected researchers with a wide variety of training. Naturally, many were in either law or anthropology, but many other disciplines were represented. Table 1 lists the final sample of research areas together with researchers, their departments and the number of extended cases collected by each. Figure 1 indicates the locations of the fieldsites.

Nearly all of the final reports are included in this volume. One researcher, Wari Iamo, who investigated customary law in Aroma, Central Province, extended his research report into a B.A. (Hons.) thesis. Since this thesis is quite extensive, and is available elsewhere (Iamoulea 1980), it has not been included in full in this collection. However, sections on marriage and land and inheritance, topics of importance in his fieldsite, have been included for representativeness in keeping with the tendency of researchers to stress topics of importance in their fieldsites.

While much diversity in customary law practices was uncovered in this research, there did appear to be some broad regional similarities in certain areas. For this reason, reports have been organized into regional groupings, although this is mainly for convenience. The four broad areas are Mainland New Guinea, New Guinea Islands, the Highlands, and Papua (excluding the Southern Highlands).

Discussion

Certain conclusions and recommendations derive from these reports and from the extended cases upon which they are based. Some of the more important of these conclusions are listed below.

1. Broad similarities in procedure rather than substance were found:

Despite the encouragement given to researchers to record standard "principles" of customary law, reports generally take the form of discussions about standard procedures followed in various types of disputes. In my own research, I often found informants unwilling to discuss cases in the abstract except in the most general terms. Many villagers are unwilling to make dogmatic statements about right and wrong, always arguing that it "depends" upon the people and circumstances involved. "Peace-keeping" rather than "administration of justice" is the aim. Conflict management takes place in moots (informal meetings for the purpose of dispute settlement). Moots differ from courts in that they have flexible rules of evidence and procedure, do not depend upon precedents or principles of **stare decisis** for their operation, and take into account personalities and situations rather than assuming that everyone is equal before the law. These basic procedures for conflict management are relatively similar throughout Papua New Guinea. In contrast, substantive law varies markedly throughout the country. This fact leads to further conclusions:

2. Because of regional diversity, extensive standardized substantive legislation is not advisable, even at the Provincial level.

Even within rather culturally homogeneous Provinces, substantive customary law varies widely. For example in Simbu province, Artihulawa reports individual ownership of land among the Siane. In East New Britain, Baining customary laws are at variance with those of the Tolai people. It would be difficult for minority cultures within a Province to follow customary rules passed by majority cultures. Thus in general, substantive standardized legislation should be approached with caution.

3. Guidelines for mediation should be developed in the form of local case law.

Although Papua New Guinea customary law does not stress the use of precedents, there are certain expectations about appropriate punishments for particular wrongs and appropriate amounts of compensation for certain actions. People generally "know" how much should be paid. these expectations have been developed through knowledge of similar cases in the past: that is, through case law. Recording of customary law cases and decisions would provide magistrates with information about what is appropriate in particular customary contexts. This information might best be recorded by appropriately trained Village Court Clerks.

4. The use of Village Courts or other bodies stressing participation, consultation and consensus should be encouraged.

Mediation and reconciliation are the bases for Papua New Guinea customary law. The Constitution calls for the use of Melanesian principles of participation, consultation and consensus. Research showed that, with a few exceptions, Village Courts are successfully integrating such principles into a western legal format. It appears that where Village Courts are not operating successfully, problems are due to lack of supervision or lack of resources rather than any structural shortcoming of the system itself. For this reason, the Village Court system should be encouraged and improved upon.

5. No general distinction between civil and criminal law was noted in Papua New Guinea.

Except for genuine cases of social deviance, often due to mental illness, most disputes in Papua New Guinea villages are considered to be "civil" in nature. A complainant has been wronged and seeks to restore economic and/or social equilibrium. This is generally accomplished through restitution or through concessions. For this reason, punishments such as compensation and community service rather than incarceration should be encouraged by the courts.

6. Broad differences were noted between Highlands and non-Highlands societies.

Relatively few broad regional patterns of any significance were noted in this research. Perhaps the most important is the general homogeneity of the Highlands region which contrasts with what might be called Lowland Papua New Guinea.

The educated Highland students writing in this volume tend to phrase customary law topics in terms of law and order and strict rules of right and wrong. In this sense, the customary law of Highlands groups is more easily codifiable. Even social groupings are more discrete, and consequently are more important in customary law.

7. Standardized legislation concerning law and order in the Highlands region is practical.

Because of the above-noted similarities, standardized legislation aimed at ameliorating law and order problems in the Highlands region is feasible. This could best be accomplished by preparing draft legislation which could then be adopted as Provincial Legislation by the five Highlands provinces. An example would be the Law Reform Commission's Report No. 11 on Customary Compensation, revised in accordance with Monograph No. 1, *Homicide Compensation in Papua New Guinea: Problems and Prospects.* Contributors to that volume pointed out some problems in non-Highland areas. Thus regional legislation would be appropriate.

8. Certain possibilities exist for substantive national legislation.

Despite the fact that substantive national legislation should be approached with caution, there are certain areas of the law where western patterns are at wide variance with Melanesian customs. These areas provide the most logical grounds for further research and subsequent legislation.

9. Land Law.

While the specifics of land law vary widely from culture to culture, there are certain similarities. In general, land is communally owned. In such cases, there is rarely total alienation of land; usufruct rights may be granted in virtual perpetuity as long as users hold to the original terms of agreement. Alienation of customary land should be discouraged, and long-term leases should be negotiated.

In general, multiple rights in land are recognized in customary law: firewood gathering rights, fishing or hunting rights, rights of thoroughfare, etc. Such rights should be recognized in law and should be clearly specified in lease agreements. The Customary Law Project is presently investigating the specifics of land law.

10. Family Law.

Western family law is based upon rather rigid monogamous patterns. Melanesian family arrangements appear to be much more flexible, and present laws appear to be serious impediments to this customary flexibility. Divorce laws in particular should be revised. Marriage laws could permit polygamy. Relatively easy registration and dissolution of customary marriages would seem to be advisable in light of project findings.

11. Contracts.

In customary law, a wide variety of social obligations exist. On the surface, some such obligations appear to be oral contracts: one party agrees to provide goods and/or services at a later date in exchange for goods or services received. Yet, in custom, such social obligations are not really binding and no real traditional mode of redress other than shame and social pressure exists. The result of habitual defaulting is a bad name and difficulties in enlisting aid. It would be incorrect to apply existing contract legislation to such situations: magistrates should clearly distinguish such practices from contracts in the western sense.

12. Torts.

Libel and slander appeared to constitute a valid indigenous forensic category virtually throughout the country. Such cases occur again and again in our corpus of extended cases. These cases should be analyzed as a separate unit to see how closely indigenous concepts of libel and slander approximate western categories, and whether revised legislation in this area would be advisable.

REFERENCES

Iamoulea, W.

1980. **Dispute Management and Social Organisation Among the Paramana People of Aroma Coast/Central Province of Papua New Guinea.** B.A. Honours Thesis, Department of Anthropology and Sociology, University of Papua New Guinea.

Law Reform Commission of Papua New Guinea

1977. **The Role of Customary Law in the Legal System.** Report No. 7, Port Moresby.

1980. **Customary Compensation.** Report No. 11, Port Moresby.

1981. **Homicide Compensation in Papua New Guinea: Problems and Prospects.** Monograph No. 1, Richard Scaglion (ed.), Port Moresby.

Scaglion, R.

1976. **Seasonal Patterns in Western Abelam Conflict Management Practices.** Ph.D. Thesis, University of Pittsburgh.

1979. Formal and informal operations of a Village Court in Maprik. **Melanesian Law Journal** 7:116-129.

1981. Samukundi Abelam conflict management: Implications for legal planning in Papua New Guinea. **Oceania** 52:28-38.

EAST PALEI

WEST SEPIK PROVINCE

Matthew Wramainiken

INTRODUCTION

The research I carried out at the end of 1979 and beginning of 1980 covered the whole East Palei electorate. It consisted of about six main languages and quite a number of dialects. Apart from that area, I also collected samples from Aitape, Nuku and Yellow River for comparison. What I found will be discussed in the contents itself. The task given was to find out as much as possible about the customary law of the area; mainly in the fields of Marriage (Family Law), Ownership, Succession and Transaction. I'll then sum up with my own generalizations.

MARRIAGE

East Palei Electorate (Nuku): I interviewed nine elders from nine villages using a systematic method. Generally speaking, what I gathered from each were all the same. The few samples from outside the field site that I took for comparison were also comparable. Basically, when the young men/women were in their teens, they were formally told about their kinship linkages. This is to avoid confusion and to avoid marrying anyone from the clan. However this word 'clan' is very peculiar, because it does not seem to be a strictly patrilineal system. In later generations, the great-grandsons/daughters of a woman could marry the great-grandsons/daughters of a brother. Specifically, we can categorise them as follows:

1. Offspring from two brothers, traced through the male line, will not intermarry for uncountable generations.

2. Similarly, offspring from two sisters will not intermarry. They will always be brothers and, if only females were born each generation,

then their children too will not intermarry.

3. A brother and sister's children, however, can intermarry after at least four generations. Refer to Figures 1.1 and 1.2 for better comprehension.

Figure 1

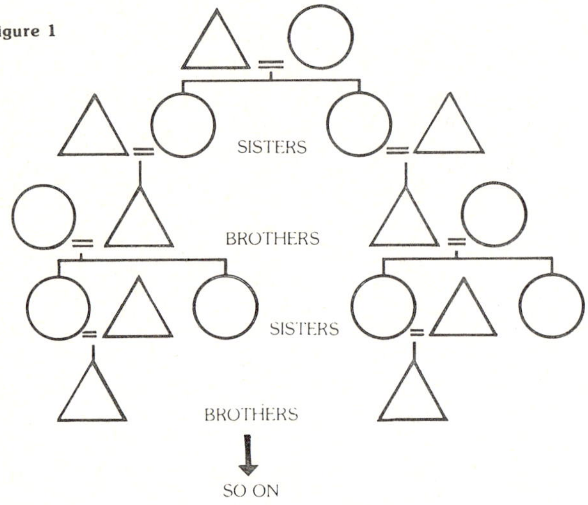

Cannot marry for uncountable generations.

Figure 2

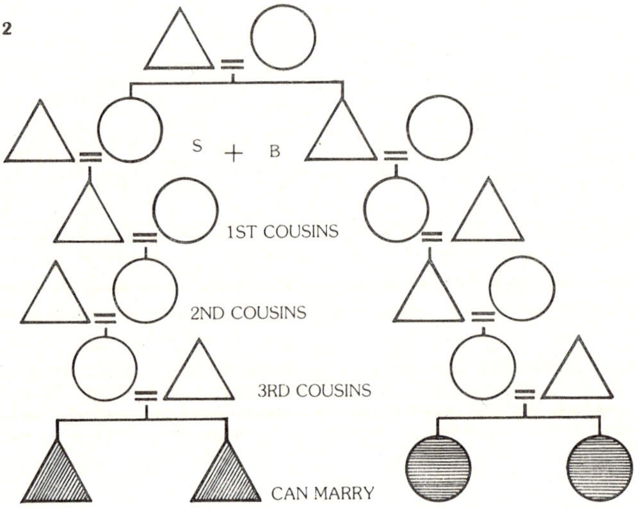

Key:

△ female

○ male

Can intermarry, but note also that the stroked △ and ○ means that from there on children can not intermarry (unless, of course if we have two different sexes from a mother or father, creating a brother-sister situation as above).

Sexual Relations:

As illustrated in Figure 1.2 above, sexual relationships should only occur between unrelated people or between people related no closer than a brother and sister's grandchildren's grandchildren. However sometimes these norms are breached as any other social norms. If so, what social sanctions would the society impose on the offender? (I'm using the singular form "offender" because it's usually the male to whom blame is attached.) There are three options depending on the characteristics of the families concerned. If the family wants compensation on the spot, then it has to be given. If not, pig meat and sprouted coconuts are exchanged. A third option is for the offender to be warned and the matter dropped. However, in this case, the offender is punished indirectly by means of such social sanctions as isolating the offender, not giving a hand in his activities when it's needed and so forth. Basically, the same principles would be imposed on persons who commit adultery. However in the case of adultery a difference could be distinguished. In the past a married man could have sexual intercourse with a single woman so long as it was not a rape and did not violate incest taboos. Today he may on occasion have to pay compensation, that is if he does not want to marry her, but usually the matter is dropped. Wives, however, cannot doublecross their husbands and go with another man, whether he be married or single. The offender would have to pay substantial compensation or the woman would be divorced and forced to marry the offender.

A single girl on her part (as the society expects) should keep away from married men and wait only for the person marked for her. Any girl who goes around with men may not find a husband. She'd be regarded as cheap and would never be faithful to her husband. However, these norms are often ignored, especially by the youth of our generation, regardless of the consequences. For example, P. was a married man, however he made a girl (who happens to be his third cousin) pregnant and she gave birth to a baby girl. P., because of breaking the kinship taboos, had to pay K100 compensation along with a pig to the girl's family. Since he was married and did not want to marry the girl, the child would have to be his responsibility. This, however, is being mixed-up with modern laws. In the past, once she was pregnant, she had to be your wife. If the girl had been promised to a boy, P. would have paid double compensation.

Bridewealth or Sister Exchange:

During my research period, I witnessed four men getting married who paid the bride price of K250 to their respective in-laws. I asked two of the girl's parents why they were getting the money, and did such a concept as "buying women" exist in the past. The answers given were, "In past marriages, we bought women with pigs and shell money. Since money has taken its place, I'd prefer money." "So you did sell your daughter after all?" I said. "I wouldn't call it that, because my daughter is not an object." The second person indicated, "I do not know why we get money as payment from our in-laws for our daughters, That, in a sense, is a sign of disposession. Our ancestors though, did give brideprice, and did not regard the concept as buying the girl. The importance of such payment was to create and maintain social relationships, and so contribute to social cohesion." He went on and said, "The simplest type of marriage is to swap sisters (sister exchange) as our forefathers did so that we would not pay large sums of money." Sister exchange was in fact the most common practice around that area. Thus for those who had no sisters, their brides were "bought" as it's called nowadays, or a female from his kin group was exchanged for his wife. However, the aspect which I think was bad was that a girl had no option but to marry whom their parents wanted. Perhaps because of family obligations or fear, most every girl in the past did what her kinsmen agreed upon.

Tabooed Relations:

Should you call your in-laws by name, it would be indeed very offending, or what is expressed as "shaming your 'tambus'". Usually you refer to them by their children's names or in case of parents-in-law, by saying your wife's father or mother. The same would apply to you. Your in-laws would address you by naming one of your children or your wife's name. This custom is found mainly around the east coast of Aitape and in the field site of Sibilanga. It may spread into all of the Nuku area, because there are already signs of it through intermarriages in some of the villages that previously had no such practice.

OWNERSHIP

In any Papua New Guinea society, how much does an individual actually own in reference to land? To the people of my fieldsite (and my area) people do not have title to land individually. Practically, land is owned on a clan basis and any fishing or hunting ground belongs solely to the clan. So do any existing resources on the land. Personally-grown fruit trees or coconuts, 'tulip' trees, betelnuts and sago are undisputed private properties. However, though land and its properties are clan-owned, a member of the clan does not require permission from elders to do things on the land. Every member can do things at will, so long as he fulfills the family obligations. That is to say, if any member has killed a pig on the clan's hunting ground, then every member has to get his share of the meat. A man's in-laws also expects things from their daughter. Approval from all other members of the clan is not required for a member to give away fruit trees, garden food, and so forth. This is called **yoki** in the local language, and will be discussed later on under "transactions."

Apart from internal members, members from other clans may have properties on the land. Obviously there is no dispute over their properties. However in some cases, land owners do demand part of whatever is produced on the land. They can also go out and fish on other people's land, but what is caught should be brought straight to the owner of the land.

Natural materials are not all that is clan owned: traditional stories and names may also be jointly owned. A name of a person, for instance, cannot be adopted into another clan, unless it is given to the child by the member of the original clan. In doing so, we have to go a step further. For example, my mother named a baby boy from another clan "Sembu", my great-grand-father's name. Since the name was ours , some fruit trees and sago palms planted by Sembu were given to him. In some cases, land would be transferred to the person bearing the name from that clan. If these things are not given then it would not be right.

Traditionally, magical stories, which are sometimes clan-owned, are not known by all the members. Elders are usually responsible for keeping these stories which are passed down in this manner from one generation to another. These are usually charms, rhythms, words for attracting women, and so forth. These nevertheless could be adopted into other clans through means of payment or friendship. For those privately owned, individuals can give them away at their own will.

Stories concerning moieties are, however, owned and known only to the clan. This is because each clan is supposed to have its own, and in fact it is through knowing these sorts of things, together with knowing ancestral rights, that properties may be safe. Otherwise another clan may cheat and rob the properties from you. To mention an example concerning ancestral rights, I refer to a 1978 case, when the land mediator was called upon to hear a quarrel between a landowner and a man who tried to build a camp on the site which had been previously used by his grandparents. After the hearing, the land mediator told the landowner to drop the matter, because as a rule, if a site was used for more than three generations without dispute, then it is rightfully the occupant's. Besides, he had properties on the land which would be accessable from the camp. But above all, the grandparents of these men had promised, by the exchange of pig meat and planting of 'tanget' to live together, and had vowed that their children would continue on with their mutual friendship. If the man had not known the story, then he would have lost the land site for his camp.

SUCCESSION

Who inherits the personal properties of a person when he/she passes away? It was possible to touch on a few of the major aspects which I'll discuss in this section. When my father died, all fruit trees and coconuts were left to my care. I was then expected to divide them among my other brothers if I wanted to. Otherwise they would be left for all of us to have equal access. These however were not shared. All my father's fruit/nut trees were left to me, because my two brothers are going to inherit our two uncles' properties, because they (the uncles) are not married and do not have any children to claim their properties. Other household properties such as pots, knives, and axes were given to my father's elder sister's daughter. Bow and arrows if he would have had any, would be given to his maternal uncles, while his clothes and other personal items were buried with him. Why his personal items are given to certain kinsmen will be elaborated under "transactions". Sometimes land or sago palms would be given to any person who cared for the sick person, or had helped him. When this happens, the properties cannot be reclaimed by the dead person's kin without payment of some sort. Not in all cases do people have relatives looking after them. Practically, this would mean any personal properties will be left only for their children, if any, otherwise to their brother's children.

In the case of women, personal properties are usually given to her nephews or nieces who were good to her. This again in the local language is called **mandiaw. Mandiaw** generally covers personal properties: including pig, 'tambu' shells and foodstuffs, which are given much later. Generally this also applies to men, and it takes palce only when a person dies. This is to put an end to the **yoki** which has been mentioned earlier.

TRANSACTIONS

As in modern systems, traditional trading or bartering does have rules. Here I'll discuss such rules in reference mainly to exchange between a man and his in-laws. The girl's brother often gives yams and bananas of a certain type, followed by a pig, to nephews and nieces. These are also often given by their aunt. Within this bartering, her/his nephews or niece are expected to give back taro (including other things like pig, coconuts, etc.) in exchange for what was given. Traditionally this is very common. Referring back to succession to a dead person's personal properties, it is these people (of course including the father's elder sister's daughters as mentioned under succession) who will inherit his personal properties.

From Figure 1.2 we find that a brother and sister's children can intermarry after at least four generations. The rule of bartering applied to that would be: you are to give the stuff mentioned above to your cousins for two generations, retire when reaching the third generation, and then start giving again if the children do intermarry during the fourth generation. This process could go on for generations, so long as they do not marry beyond that boundary.

Another type of bartering is coconuts in exchange for coconuts. This occurs when somebody from a village dies and they decide to stop getting coconuts. In this case I'll refer to 1975, when my village, Yanungen, received their payment from Parkop. Lightning struck two brothers from Parkop, so they decided to stop getting their coconuts, and looked instead to Yanungen for all their supply for two years. After all the nuts sprouted and all the trees had nuts, they had to make repayment. I should mention here, too, that people from Parkop had to choose their respective partners, who were usually their distant relatives as well. So when we went down to get our coconuts, we went straight to our partners, who had already prepared things for us. That, however, as it's termed, is for "the house". For Yanungen Village as a whole is filled up outside with those provided for the neighbouring or visiting villages. The foodstuffs I should mention included betelnuts, sprouted and unsprouted coconuts and all other types of food. These however, as a rule, were given in the morning after Yanungen and some other visiting villages had staged ceremonies for the whole night.

The **wuyam,** which is similar to the practice described above, is based on pig exchange. While it is for a different purpose, it follows the same pattern and includes the same foodstuffs. **Wuyam** usually occur to ensure friendship or further strengthen ties with a neighbouring village which had shown support in a fight or saved somebody, etc. For such cases, well over 60 pigs or so are given and have to be paid back accordingly. Precisely this sort of exchange is usually permanent and is carried out each generation. Some villages may have two partners. It is during these times that a person is able to get bows, clay pots, armbands and so forth which are requested from a person of an exchange village. It is considered very embarrassing to just give these items in a non-ceremonial context to a person from a village which is your partner in pig exchange.

Such exchanges usually start off with an individual family, who then recruit others and make it as a village matter. How would one feel even though he's from a different clan or moiety when he doesn't help? A saying often used goes, "Look up to others and they'll see you. Look down, and you are on your own." So even though the matter may originally concern only one person, every other associated person is obliged to help.

Normal individual bartering happens anytime. So long as you have something you want to give in exchange for whatever item, you can go and exchange it with anyone. So long as you do not violate the rules (i.e. like not cheating, telling lies, etc.) one of your partners may become a permanent trading agent which may then lead to **wuyam.**

GENERALIZATION

Juding from what I've witnessed and the samples I've collected, different traditional laws from Aitape area. Lumi and Nuku area do not contrast, though there may be slight differences, which I do not take into account. Further investigation would have to be carried out before we could be sure that they are comparable. Such customary laws are also applicable in parts of the East Sepik Province especially the areas which have close cultural contacts with the areas researched. This may be true in other parts of West Sepik and East Sepik, though it is true that there may be great differences, particularly in the area of Succession and Transactions. Generally speaking, marriage patterns seem most similar.

AMAHOP (Balif) ARAPESH

EAST SEPIK PROVINCE

Raymond Kamanabi

INTRODUCTION

The aims of this research were first; as a short term objective, to give the student researcher an opportunity to practice the learned skills in a real working situation; and second, as a long term objective, to provide data for the Law Reform Commission to be able to develop a national legal system that would be acceptable to the people of Papua New Guinea. I carried out my field work research in Amahop village, situated on the Sepik highway about 8 kilometers west of Maprik town. The village is segmented into Amahop Nos. 1, 2 and 3 (further down) and together, has an estimated population of about 1,000 or more. Amahop is classified as a village belonging to the Balif — Arapesh dialect within the Southern Arapesh group of the Toricelli phylum (Tuzin 1975:55). One of the reasons for choosing this village as the target of research is because of its location near the border of Abelam, the customary law of whom was previously studied by Scaglion (1979, 1981). Consequently, it would be interesting to find out its correlations and interactions across the border. The following then are the findings from the research done during the period November 1979 to February 1980, on customary law practices in the community as representative of the Arapesh culture.

THE WORK SITUATION

Before moving on to discuss the various findings as outlined, I would like to mention the kind of activity undertaken, work skills gained, problems encounted, and the success and failures that I faced during the research. Briefly, the kind of activities undertaken were interviewing, observation and case study. By case study, it is meant here the use of records of previous cases held by appropriate authorities like the Welfare Office. The three most important skills that I gained in the field were the ability to translate, note-taking, and listening. To translate here means the ability to translate correctly into Tok Pisin and the local dialect for effective communication and answers. To be able to take notes at a required speed and listen at the same time is a great task for any researcher. I believe that a good researcher learns more by listening than by paying greater attention to note-taking.

Apart from family obligations, bad weather and other limitations, the only problem I faced was that of misunderstandings resulting from Tok Pisin use of kinship terminologies by those interviewed. This meant that we would spend a lot of time determining the right relationship of the interviewee to the others in question. For example, 'brata' means both brother or sister and not 'brata' for brother. In the more common usage, people could be heard to say 'brata' either way and not 'brother or sister'.

Although I could not find out as much as I wanted to, the reseach on the whole was successful largely due to the acceptance (of me), co-operation, assistance and patience of the people. Besides, it was a first time for such research to be done in the community and the people showed interest in the work, compared to those in my original location (Roma). I can not pinpoint any specific failures but appointments were thought to be at times a problem because I turned up either early or late or that the interviewee had gone out due to some unexpected reasons. In this case, we had to agree on another suitable time. On the other hand, and to be frank, the only failure of this work is that of my failure to make available this report as soon as required – not only because of the work load but also the many personal problems that had me depressed and unhappy. This is something that future students in the programme should learn to avoid. Let us then proceed now to look at some of the findings of the research.

LAND

As in other Papua New Guinea societies, land is regarded as the source of life and wealth by Amahop villagers. Today, it is even more important to a village that is facing increasing land shortages as its population accelerates over the years. Let us then look at some of the customary law practices concerning land.

Ownership:

Like the Abelam (Scaglion 1976:65) land is found to be owned by the lineage. There is no individual ownership except in the case where a man had cleared away a section of land for the first time without help from other relatives. In addition, there are other pieces of land that are jointly owned by the lineages or the community as a whole. The latter actually applies to land communally owned such as hunting grounds, for instance.

Land Tenure:

Although a man can have ownership title to pieces of land and make his own choice as to the use of a piece of land, nevertheless the head(s) of the lineage usually have ultimate rights over the use of the land for whatever purposes. This means that permission, as a requirement, must be sought even by the father's own sons to garden the land, stating reasons for wanting to use that land at that time. Also, any person wishing to plant a coconut tree, for example, on another man's land must seek the consent of the owner first. Otherwise, the owner has the right to destroy it. Furthermore, rights to coconuts, sago palms, fruit trees and other food plants belong to the original planter or the lineage where communal ownership is predominant. Interesting is the fact that reclaimation of any property by the land owner depends on the agreement between him and the planter.

Inheritance:

For the most part, Amahop is a patrilineal society in which inheritance of land is automatically passed from father to sons, or to the eldest sister in the case where there are no sons in the family. If a father dies, the eldest son takes his place as the head of the family and directs its activities. Sometimes, where there are no children born into a family, problems arise as to who should have this and that if the deceased spouses had not distributed their property and land to relatives of their preference.

Hunting and Fishing:

In the past, there were no rules regarding hunting and fishing at the village level. But at the inter-village level, it was stated that people from another village were not allowed to trespass on the village's hunting and fishing grounds. However, they say that all this has now changed with the advent of western laws and the Village Court. Today, nobody is to tread on other people's land without prior consent or without a reasonable excuse.

OWNERSHIP AND PROPERTY

In this second section, we shall look at songs/names, personal and family property, and theft as some of the aspects of rights to ownership and use of property.

Songs and Names:

It was stated that exclusive rights to ownership and use of songs and names belong only to the lineage or clan concerned. Anyone outside the lineage wanting to use a name or sing songs at a special occasion must seek permission beforehand. Names here do not mean the names of individuals, but rather, the names of clans — for instance, the **wama** clan (or 'pisin'), **wama** meaning the white cockatoo.

Personal and Family Property:

Much can be said in this area, but briefly, exclusive rights to ownership and use of property belong to the individuals, in the case of individual ownership, or the family, in the case of family ownership. Personal property can be things like clothes, gardening tools and weapons. On the other hand, family property includes those things that members jointly own, such as coconut trees, sago palms, and domestic animals. In each case, consent of the owner is essential if another person wishes to have access to that property. For the family (or lineage), consent is usually sought from the head of the family. Furthermore, where borrowing takes place without prior consultation, the rule is that the owner should be notified as soon as possible. Failing to do so would be regarded as stealing.

Theft of Property:

Stealing is an offence and people found to be stealing can face verbal or physical confrontation with the owner and his relatives. The principles involving theft of property are few but the three that seem to emerge are:

1. Removal or claim without owners' knowledge is unlawful.
2. Compensation must be made when rights are violated.
3. Verbal warfare and forgiveness occur where close relatives are involved.

AUTHORITY AND POWER

It is felt that authority and power play a vital role in creating harmony and stability of the community. This is witnessed in Amahop and Arapesh villages where the motto 'together as a group' and not as an 'individual' in the community is most predominant. However, evidence from the research seems to suggest a defined leadership pattern. Here, leadership and control seem to be in the hands of influential big men and not all the big men. Interviewing the big men on the various subjects is perhaps the best example to illustrate the above point. Many referred me to others either because they did not know much about the subject or they felt that they were not important enough to receive me.

Leadership Succession:

Unlike the Trobriands practice, succession to leadership is one of achievement and is not ascribed. It is worth mentioning that the son of a big man is already an important person in the village, but this should not mean that he is already a big man. Depending on his personality, he may be recognised as a potential leader, but then he has to prove himself as a leader and be accepted as one by the community.

Warfare and Alliance:

Warfare and alliance also play an important role in the life and stability of the community. Historically, more than half the villages are descendants of forefathers who had migrated and settled into the area. Like others, they have to fight off external aggression and establish themselves permanently in the community. Once again, authority to lead and negotiate are the responsibilities of the influential big men.

Cases 1101 and 1109 on land disputes are examples that show the influence of the big men in this area. In case 1109, it is interesting to note that one of the reasons for allowing another group to settle on one's land is really to aid the host community in warfare.

RITUAL LIFE

In this section, we shall look at some of the aspects of the ritual life of the Amahop dwellers. It would be difficult to cover much detail in such a small space so I shall only detail the underlying principles of customary law in this area.

Yam Institution:

Firstly, it is thought that the yam institution was adopted from the Abelam people by the Arapesh owing to the "--- mass of beliefs and ritual practices currently surrounding yam production and competition" (Tuzin 1972:79). Basically, the underlying principles of the institution as evident from interviews and discussions are: power, prestige and strength. The politics of yams can be best described as fighting with food (as elsewhere) to attain power, prestige and strength both at the village and inter-village levels. The two principal yams grown are **ujimbu** and **mambutap.** The latter is grown some months after the former and is the most important of the two. It is a demanding institution in which all kinds of rules (or taboos) have to be observed by the grower and the community at large such as:–

1. prohibition of sexual intercourse with wives by growers
2. women and children not allowed to enter the garden
3. eating of certain meats by the grower prohibited
4. foreigners not allowed into the garden.

Such regulations (or taboos), similar to those of the Samukundi Abelam (Scaglion 1978, Scaglion and Condon 1979), are essential to safeguard the growth of the yams and the wellbeing of the grower(s). Usually, members of a ward or moiety cultivate together and not with members of other moieties.

'Tambaran':

Secondly, it is also believed that the 'tambaran' cult was superimposed on a pre-existing initiation system of the Arapesh and is a religious institution that is more appropriate to larger villages than to dispersed hamlets" (Tuzin 1976:79). Again the underlying principles of the cult are power, prestige, and strength, largely at the group level within and outside the village. I shall not enter into any detailed discussion, as much of the beliefs and practices are similar to that of the Abelam. In short, evidence seems to suggest that most of the activity is centered around the initiation of youth (namely males) as adult member of the community.

There are three types of 'tambaran': **ul'pe, memainabe** (both female 'tambarans') and **gwwaldu** (male 'tambaran'). The last is the most important one that takes place after the other two. Usually, the cult involves competition between two or more clans, not individuals, except in cases where individual rivalry arises and forces relatives to take sides. Initiation is the process in which the youth goes through to be officially, if I may say, recognised and accepted as an adult member of the community. For the males, it is not a compulsory requirement but for the females, it is a different case in which initiation is a tradition that takes place at the first menstruation.

Menstruation:

Unlike the Abelam, the taboos on menstruation are not so diverse and rigid so as to supress the freedom of movement by women during menstruation.

However the Amahop people do share the common beliefs that menstruation is unclean and dangerous to health and growth of food and people, and must be treated with caution.

Pregnancy and Childbirth:

I was unable to establish any concrete facts about pregnancy and childbirth, but it is felt that the rules are many and complex. Sexual intercourse during pregnancy and breast feeding is prohibited for fear of damaging the growth of the child and for another unwanted conception. After a period of one to two years or more when the child is walking then the parents can sleep together again. In some instances, women not wanting to have babies can take traditional drugs to stop them from conceiving. However, again consent is required from the husband (in the case of married couples) or the mother (in the case of young females).

The general underlying principles of childbirth are first, to have children to inherit land and property; second, for labour (manpower); and third, for the care of parents at old age.

Sorcery and Witchcraft:

The underlying principles of sorcery and witchcraft here are: protection, and imposing negative sanctions against the deviants. By protection, it is meant here the use of sorcery to safeguard the interests of the practitioner, his family and thereby, the lineage he belongs to. Witchcraft, in the magical context, is a means for destroying or healing the sick. Interesting is the fact that the institution of 'sanguma' (sorcery) does not actually exist in Amahop Arapesh. However, individuals can negotiate with the so-called 'sangumas' of 'sanguma - practicing villages to destroy their foes. However, this is not the common practice, since the use of 'sanguma' is a threat to the existence of the village as a whole in the long run. It was expressed that excessive or unreasonable use of sorcery and witchcraft is a threat to the welfare of the community. Therefore, the Amahop villagers spend more time trying to prevent the use of sorcery than to impose any negative sanctions. Negative sanctions are imposed only when disputes leading to grievances arise.

Death:

When a man dies without any physical signs of being naturally sick, the people are ready to reach one conclusion as to the cause of death: and that can be either sorcery or 'sanguma' or witchcraft.

If that happens, three main events take place at the same time:

1. Rights of relatives to see the body before burial are respected.
2. A public forum is held to determine the cause of death, and
3. Feasts/ceremonies are held to minimize future disputes.

It worth remembering that as an institution, death is a continual process that involves the displacement, re-organization and re-socialization of those affected and in the case of big men, of the community as a whole.

Hunting:

Before the influences of Abelam intrusion were felt, the Arapesh economy was based on sago and hunting and gathering (Tuzin 1976:70). Hunting was essential in the past in that meat had to be provided at feasts since pig breeding was not as intensive as it is in other societies. One reason being that in those days, there were abundant meat resources in the bush. With the introduction of the shotgun, however, most if not all meat has become scarce and difficult to find. Like others, the people of this village believe that hunting is a secret thing where hunters must not tell others about the hunt. By not letting their intentions be known, the hunters can assume safely that the spirits of the forests have not warned the game away.

Deviance:

Deviance is herein defined as the turning away from the principles of thesocial and political system of a society. In Amahop, people who deviate from the cultural norms and values are subjected to negative sanctions or face expulsion by the community. For example, a one-time witchcraft practitioner was expelled from the community because he was considered to be dangerous to the community and he now lives by himself about two kilometers away in a lonely location.

SEX AND PROHIBITED RELATIONSHIPS

Sex outside of marriage is not prohibited but nevertheless, it is a serious matter that must be treated with precautions to safeguard the interests of the individuals and the community (Mead 1963:99).

Premarital Sex:

Strictly speaking, what is meant here is sex before marriage by the youth. There is no set age but as expressed, early contact (especially the males) can be dangerous to the growth and social stability of the youth.

For example, early contact can arouse unwanted desires that may lead the youth into aggressive sexual advances on both the married and unmarried women.

Fornication:

In regard to the question of fornication, it was stated that outside marriage, there are no taboos so long as there was no alienation of affection between the adult partners. It is my assumption that fornication may be a contributing factor to increased population in societies that do not prohibit such relationships. However, in this case, the rationale is not a romantic but a domestic one (Mead 1963:99) for reasons that are discussed in the section on pregnancy and childbirth.

Other Sexual Offences:

Rape. Theoretically, rigidly-sanctioned relationships allow chances of rape occuring to be remote, although the dangers of rape do not need to be pointed out. I was not able to establish any concrete facts, but from observation and discussions, it was evident that rape could have been an adopted practice, which has had the tendency to increase as the society changed to a modern society that allows freedom of movement, thoughts and action.

Homosexuality. There is no homosexuality in Amahop. If there is evidence of such a practice, it may have been due to the result of external influences.

Battery and slander. Although the usage here is not in terms of biological contact, false statements or untrue stories about one's sexual activities (or life) can often lead to prolonged major disputes, assault and food fighting. People found in the act of creating social disruptions are liable to compensate those injured and if not, can face negative social sanctions. The Village Court has recognised this and numbers 2, 3, 5 and 6 of the Offences set out in the Handbook for Village Court Officers (1976:25) can be applied. I shall explore a bit more on the question of sex in the following section.

FAMILY LAW

Much can be said here but due to limitation of space I would like to discuss only some of the main issues of family law practices in Amahop.

Age and Parental Consent:

Firstly, there is no set age for marriage. Marriage is on the basis of physical maturity. For the females, marriage can take place any time after the first menstruation. However, in the past, child betrothal was a common practice in which actual marriage was the physical union of the spouses after the initiation of the woman. Since most marriages were arranged by parents and close relatives, parental consent was not generally necessary. This means that the question of consent is not parental but that of the young spouses that may often be persuaded to accept the marriage arrangement.

Bridewealth:

It was stated that bridewealth is not the practice in Amahop. Where a woman was from another village, rings, yams and meat had to be paid as compensation to the close relatives for the loss of their sister to another village. Today, owing to external influences and the rapidly changing social and political system, bridewealth has now become a common practice in Amahop. However, in numerical terms, the money demanded as brideprice does not exceed K1000.00 as compared to other places.

Marriage and Dissolution of Marriage:

Potential spouses are usually considered married when the female enters the house of the male or his parents (where the husband has no house of his own) and are sleeping together. In the past, if couples (either one or both) refused the proposed marriage, they would be locked up separately in a house to give them the opportunity to explore and accept each other.

The common type of marriage was arranged marriage or brother-sister exchange marriage. If a brother had no sister, then his family, and thereby the lineage, was in debt to the lineage from which the woman came. As stated, marriage is not complete without traditional ceremony. Briefly, when a marriage takes place, an exchange feast is held for a period of one week in which sisters support the female and the brothers support the male. After the one week is over, the newlyweds are allowed to wash up and go out of their brief seclusion to their new home. A couple can be expected to start life with nothing more than a few personal belongings. However, the custom in Amahop is that at the beginning, yams, 'mamis' and material property (e.g. coconut trees) are allocated to help the couple to become self-sufficient and contributors in the long run. Dissolution of marriages is a difficult task but can be possible, depending on the mediation between all the parties concerned. As stated, dissolution is only allowed where spouses are not able to live together in peace and harmony due to interpersonal or external factors.

Sexual Rights:

The underlying principle is that sexual rights belong only to the husband. When they are violated, he has a right to demand compensation or, for many, physical confrontation. For instance, whilst adultery is a wrong-doing, it is also considered as stealing another person's wife or husband. When a husband or wife takes the latter view, physical confrontation or yam competition involving lineages of the competitors takes place.

Polygyny and Polyandry:

In the marriage structure, monogamy is presumed but polygyny is permitted in which a man may (if he is able) have two or more wives to make his life easier. With regard to polyandry, the Amahop Arapesh do not have such an institution, and it is considered a new alien concept to them.

Adoption:

Before we move on to the next topic, I would like to briefly discuss some of the aspects of adoption in the Amahop community. Firstly, fostering is only allowed within a defined circle — meaning here the close relatives only. Fostering of children usually occurs when couples have no children and desire someone to inherit their land and property after their death. Secondly, care of orphans follows the same general pattern described for fostering, except that sometimes, the orphan may be rejected by the community for various reasons and would have to provide his own maintenance. Thirdly, children are the sole responsibility of the mother, although in many instances when others are able to marry, the children are accepted by the husband as his own for reasons I have stated earlier for having children. Next, guardianship is again the same as that in fostering. However, in the case of widows, a widow can, after a certain length of time, either remarry or remain independent for the rest of her life.

For example, Yariva had been worried for some time that Alubuli, who was already married, had been making sexual advances with the intention to marry her. During heated exchanges, it was decided that there would be no marriage as Yariva was still mourning over the loss of her husband and did not wish to marry again. Remarriage of widows, then, is a sensitive issue that demands a lot of mediation and subsequently, feasts and other minor compensation to minimize future disputes.

HOUSING AND RESIDENCE

From observations, it was seen that the type of houses built in the village are open or closed pyramids, but compared to those of the Abelam, are bigger in size and height. Houses raised above the ground and houses with thatched 'morata' (sago leaves) are not traditional. Although rights to housing and housing locations belong to the individual or the family, certain provisions exist to restrict the type of houses a man can build. A big man, for instance, can build a house of any type, but a young man cannot do so, if he had not seen the 'tambaran' (been initiated). Today, many of these restrictions have been relaxed as a result of western influences and Christianity.

Residential location is largely a patrilineal rather than a matrilineal choice. Often matrilineal choice occurs when a man is rejected by his close family and is forced to live in his wife's home for reasons such as continual land disputes and ill feelings. In addition, it was expressed that members of a family or lineage can only settle on land belonging to the lineage and cannot settle on other people's land. If a man wishes to settle on another man's land, he must consult and obtain the owner's permission. Otherwise, it would be considered illegal squatting. Sometimes a man can live in seclusion from the rest of the community if he so wishes, but still has his obligations to the community.

SOCIAL OBLIGATIONS

Social obligations, it can be said, are one of the strengths of the traditional society in its continual social and political functioning. In Amahop their significance can be seen in the daily activities of the people where labour or work organization is based on the "group" ideology.

Respect and Responsibility:

It is a general principle that children should respect their parents, and parents have a duty to bring up their children to be creative members of the community. Elders are the sources of authority and power and must be respected at all times. All members of the community except those under ten years of age have the responsibility to work and support the family and thereby the community. At the inter-group level, families formed by marriage have the responsibility to support each other when requested for work and in times of trouble.

Rights and Duties:

Interestingly, rights by individuals and families to demand, expect, perform or take action are recognised as essential to the welfare of the community. For example, parents in old age have the right to expect their children to look after them. After all, the principle of child bearing is for this purpose. When they die, other people cannot bury their bodies because if this happened, the children would be required to compensate the work done by others.

As a rule, if a person looks after another in old age, either because he has no children or the children do not wish to care for him, then the person taking care of the elderly person has the right to inherit some or all the land and property owned by the deceased.

Following on, for those who are required to help when requested, it is their duty to uphold these obligations. Failure to do so could mean that disputes would arise sooner or later and could mean the loss of future obligations to those concerned by others. Also, it is the duty of all to observe the many taboos that the community has, particularly the ritual life of the villagers. For example, women should not step over old men and children, or eat in the same plate or pot, as these may endanger the welfare of the old and the growth of children. Disputes can also arise when one does not uphold these duties expected from him/her.

DISPUTE SETTLEMENT

Before concluding the discussion I shall look at some of the aspects of dispute settlement. Basically, the two main principles as stated are: first, to maintain social harmony, peace and stability of the community; and second, to establish superiority over rivals for recognition and strength. Primarily, dispute settlement was the task of the big men who could, for days or months, mediate for a solution that would be acceptable to all. The types of dispute settlements can range from individual matters to matters beyond the village level. The ideal settlement pattern involves mediation, compensation and exchange feasts. Meat, yams and food plus shell rings (depending on the circumstance) form compensation payments where disputes arise between villages. Case 1109, a land dispute between Amahop and a neighbouring Abelam village (Kulelikum), is an example of such a settlement. It is worth remembering that dispute settlements are difficult and often prolonged when grievances and counter-grievances occur. Indeed, it is a non-stop process that can give rise to complications when past settlements are used as reference to the present ones. Breaches of any agreements both at the village and inter-village levels are serious, and negative sanctions can be exercised.

CONCLUSION

To conclude, it may be said that the Amahop (Arapesh)culture is an importing culture (Mead 1938, Tuzin 1976:79). This conclusion is reinforced by the fact that Amahop shares a common border with the Abelam villages (Aupik, Yamelikum and Kulelikum). Consequently, many of its customary law practices are similar as a result of interaction across the border. However, there are differences that sometimes the villagers themselves may not be aware of when comparison with other societies arise. Some of these differences can be outlined as follows:

1. sex and prohibited relationships,
2. ritual life (e.g. menstruation, death),
3. sorcery and witchcraft (sanguma),
4. labour organization in gardening and other work,
5. family law (bridewealth and polygyny),
and so on.

From this and many other similar research studies, and considering the few differences, it can be argued that a common but moderate legal system can be developed that would be acceptable to the people. However, when we go out from the Provincial level, problems arise when different cultures of other provinces conflict with ours. This, I am afraid, is the greatest difficulty the Law Reform Commission would face in its efforts to formulate an acceptable national legal system. Furthermore, it was found that dispute settlements today in the Village Court seem to be more western-oriented than traditional. Asked why this was so, it was stated that money is easier to acquire and repay at short notice. But the traditional compensation system (involving pigs, yams and rings) is a demanding task that often takes a long time to finally settle a dispute. Lastly, I have no recommendations to make but would like to say that such an experience (made possible by the Commission and the social work programme) is a valuable asset to the student whereby he is (as a potential researcher) better equipped in the field of social research as he leaves the University to enter into the outside world.

Table 2.1

PRINCIPAL INFORMANTS

1. Barnabas	Amahop No. 1	Area Pastor & Big Man
2. Bina Maga	Amahop No. 2	Village Court Peace Officer
3. Dua Duguadu	Amahop No. 2	Big Man
4. James Amibuan	Amahop No. 1	Village Court Clerk
5. John Kunbango	Amahop No. 1	Councillor
6. Kumun Siale	Amahop No. 1	Big Man
7. Lanis	Amahop No. 2	Host

Table 2.2

SUBSTANTIVE LAW OUTLINE: AMAHOP (Balif) ARAPESH

1. INTERPERSONAL CONFLICTS.
   (a) Disputes over women
   (b) Conflicts over domestic animals
   (c) Disputes over ownership and use of property
   (d) Other Domestic Arguments

2. INTERGROUP CONFLICTS.
   (a) As in (1) above (at a group level)
   (b) Authority and Power
   (c) Fighting
   (d) Food (Production, Distribution and Consumption)

3. FAMILY LAW
   (a) Marriage
   (b) Dissolution of Marriage
   (c) Sexual Rights
   (d) Marital Property Rights
   (e) Bridewealth
   (f) Parent-Child
   (g) Widowhood

4. BREACHES OF CUSTOMARY LAW
   (a) 'Tambaran'
   (b) Yams
   (c) Land Ownership and Use
   (d) Inheritance
   (e) Sorcery and Witchcraft (Sanguma)
   (f) Theft
   (g) Social Obligations
   (h) Ritual Taboos
   (i) Permission of Owners

5. DISPUTE SETTLEMENT
   (a) Community Mediation by Big Men
   (b) Compensation to the Injured
   (c) Fighting with Food (and Meat)
   (d) Probation (or Expulsion)
   (e) Breaches of past Agreements

REFERENCES

Mead, M.

1963. **Sex and Temperament in Three Primitive Societies.** Morrow, New York.

Scaglion, R.

1976. **Seasonal Patterns in Western Abelam Conflict Management Practices.** Ph.D. Thesis, University of Pittsburgh.

1978. Seasonal births in a western Abelam village, Papua New Guinea. **Human Biology** 50:313-323.

1979. Formal and informal operations of a Village Court in Maprik. **Melanesian Law Journal** 7:116-129.

1981. Samukundi Abelam conflict management: implications for legal planning in Papua New Guinea. **Oceania** 52:28-38.

Scaglion R. and R.G. Condon.

1979. Abelam yam beliefs and sociorhythmicity: a study in chronoanthropology. **Journal of Biosocial Science** 11:17-25.

Tuzin, D.F.

1976. **The Ilahita Arapesh: Dimensions of Unity.** University of California Press.

MAMBE AREA

EAST SEPIK PROVINCE

Tarcissius Muganaua

INTRODUCTION

The Law Reform Commission of Papua New Guinea has been trying its best in reviewing some of the laws of the land to meet the needs and aspirations of the people and indeed there has been some achievement. This paper contributes to its investigations with particular focus on customary law development. Thus the theme for my discussion is, "Customary Law Practices: An Analysis of the Research Findings in the Mambe Court Area from the 16th November 1979 to the 8th of February 1980".

The objectives of the research are twofold. The short term objective is to provide the Law Reform Commission with some of the customary law principles from my area, thus fulfilling the given task of collecting data. The long term objective is for the Commission to see whether some of these principles of customary law can be reviewed and introduced (if applicable) to meet the Papua New Guinean situation by fulfilling the fifth National Goal as stated in the Constitution, "Papua New Guinean Ways".

Location of the Area:

The Mambe Court area is in Turubu, a constituency in the Wewak District. It is south-south-east of Wewak town while to the east-south-east and northwest are the districts of Angoram and Maprik. The area is situated on fertile hill sides, surrounded by parts of the Prince Alexander ranges and the beautiful overview of the Sepik plains in the South. The villages that make up the Court area are Mambe, Manuana, Yamben, Parpur, Turureru 1, Turureru 2 and Numbingo; with an estimated population of 3,200 people.

Economic development in the area includes individual and group ownership of trade stores, PMVs, and cash cropping; individual cash farming (cocoa, coffee, rice); and cattle projects, piggery, poultry and buffalo all on a village basis. Although commercial activity is becoming more common, subsistence economy remains the major source of livelihood and surely the surplus becomes another source of income.

There has been considerable improvement in the living standards of people as a result of the accessibility of social services such as aid posts, educational facilities, Maternal Child Health Clinics and visiting nurses who teach mothers about hygiene.

The Methodology of the Research:

The two methods used during the research were interviewing and observation. Much of my interviewing took place during the evenings because that seemed to be the only possible time in meeting my informants. Rarely did I make it during the day. Most often I did a follow-up interview if I had doubts or uncertainties over misleading information on a particular subject. Only on two occasions have I used the observation method, one while witnessing a case on sorcery and the other on a domestic argument between householders. It is more useful in the sense that it gives you firsthand information about the whole affair.

With this particular research, skills were not a very big problem. In this case, communication was very important and, in order to communicate effectively, one has to know his own (local) language. It was discovered in the field that note-taking is necessary and should be given priority too, only when the circumstances allow. For my case, notes were taken in rough form and then put in proper form later.

I played the role of a researcher throughout the whole study period, although apart from this, I played a number of roles particularly when I was involved with community work. As a researcher, I was more concerned with the immediate task of collecting data and sending it in an interim report to my fieldwork supervisor.

Limitations:

In the course of carrying out this task, a number of problems were seen as an obstacle to the overall study. The most obvious of all was family obligations and commitments. The fact is you cannot be totally independent as a student at the University of Papua New Guinea. You must follow, comply with and appreciate the fact that you are in, or faced with, another sphere of life which is seen as more important. At times when I was supposed to be travelling to a village, I got held up by my parents or relatives to do this and that for them. I had to feel committed most of the time.

The second was one of community involvement, particularly with the Boys Town activity. Being a close member to the congregation of the Sacred Hearts Brothers, I was much inclined to serve the community in one way or another. During this period of study, I was asked voluntarily to see whether I could offer assistance in their daily routine activities, obviously due to shortage of staff. Indeed, I have found the experience quite worthwhile. By living in Boys Town, I had easy access to telephone use at the Provincial Office, lights to complete interim reports during night time, and other closer necessities as well for my field work.

The third obstacle was of case study with various cases written about each court area. When reaching the supervisory magistrate responsible, I was informed that the data were not up to date in a standardised manner. However I was permitted to go through some of the cases and did discover a few cases from my own area. Much of the manner in which it was structured was too legalistic, and actually difficult to analyse.

The fourth obstacle was both weather and illness. Sometimes it rained so heavily that I had to stop travelling to the villages I had planned to visit initially. At other times my visits had to stop because of illness. I could have covered more during the three weeks that I was sick.

Table 3.1

UNDERLYING PRINCIPLES IN CUSTOMARY LAW

CUSTOMARY PRACTICE — MAMBE COURT AREA

1. LAND	
(a) Ownership	Lineage or clan at large.
(b) Land tenure	Rights/consultation — approved from heads of lineage.
(c) Inheritance	Father to sons (daughters).
(d) Hunting and fishing	Rights by family.
2. OWNERSHIP AND PROPERTY	
(a) Songs and names	Lineage/clan.
(b) Personal property	Individual.

(c) Family property	Family consultation/approval.
(d) Theft	(a) Removal claim without owner's knowledge is unlawful. (b) Forgiveness (compensation).
3. AUTHORITY AND POWER	
(a) Leadership and control	Recognised 'Big' men.
(b) Leadership succession	Achieved.
(c) Warfare and alliances	Recognised influential 'Big' men.
4. HOUSING AND RESIDENCE	
(a) Types of housing	Flexible.
(b) Housing provisions	Flexible with few exceptions.
(c) Residential location	On land belonging to lineage/moiety but with little exception.
(d) Residential status	Flexible.
5. SOCIAL OBLIGATIONS	
(a) Respect and responsibility	Varied examples — care for the old/care for the sick.
(b) Rights and duties	As observe by society — initiative.
6. SEX	
(a) Pre-marital sex	Dangerous to growth.
(b) Fornication	Strictly prohibited.
(c) Incest	Biologically unintentional.
(d) Other sexual offences e.g. homosexuality; rape	High secretive between individuals involved but no specific case (to reseacher's understanding).
7. FAMILY LAW	
(a) Age	Puberty — Initiation.
(b) Bride wealth	To relatives.
(c) Exchange marriage	Brother — sister basis.
(d) Dissolution/divorce	Mediation by parties concerned.
(e) Adultery	(a) Unlawful (b) Compensation.
(f) Polygamy	Individual choice.
(g) Remarriage of widows	Through mediation.
(h) Adoption	
i) Fostering	Within a defined group.
ii) Orphanage	Lineage.
iii) Illegitimate child	Mother's responsibility.
iv) Guardianship	Immediate relatives.
v) Widows	Immediate relatives/independent care.
8. RITUAL LIFE	
(a) Menstruation	Unclean and dangerous to growth and health.
(b) Sorcery/witchcraft	Protection/Sanction.
(c) Death	a) Rights of relatives to see before burial. b) Ceremony after burial. c) Identify cause of death before burial.
(d) Initiation	All youth should be initiated.
(e) Hunting	Individually/collectively — secrecy involved.

PRINCIPLES OF CUSTOMARY LAW

Table 3.1 summarizes some of the underlying principles in customary law which are customary practices throughout the Mambe Court area. The following will be paragraphs of explanation concerning the information summarized in tabular form.

The principal law regarding land ownership is communal (lineage or clan) ownership. When disputes arise out of a land issue, it means for sure that someone has no legal right over the land, and therefore the complainant has every right to appeal for justice through the Village Courts.

With regard to land tenure, elderly men from the lineage are responsible for approval of rights, consultation matters, etc. Sometimes elderly women are involved with the consultation and approval of rights, especially if they have lived longer than their male counterparts, and can determine who inherits which piece of land.

The present practice regarding inheritance of land is one of 'father to son' and it will most likely continue to be a practice in the future. However there is an exception, where a daughter is eligible to inherit if there is no male member in the family, provided that she will marry within the paternal boundary. In other words, she has to marry from within the village so that she could take possession of all the inherited property.

The underlying principle for hunting and fishing ownership is bestowal to family groups, which may also include those members of closely extended families as well. Sometimes the members of the one lineage carry out collective activities so that the catch could then be shared equally among every householder. However, if the catch is not plentiful, then normally the older people and widows would be the immediate receivers.

The notion of retaining pride and patriotism within one's lineage or clan is important, and songs and names play a significant part in customary law. The idea of superiority-inferiority statuses can come about in the form of drama or folkore if one lineage exhibits much more than the other groups during social gatherings. It's a very competitive thing to a large extent, having components of customs and emblems.

Total ownership of individual and family property is the general principle, however it can be loosely described in actual practice. In other words, the whole community has respect towards one another in a family type atmosphere so that when a close relative takes anything such as firewood, an implement, or a bunch of bananas from a garden, the owner will already have worked out roughly who did this and that. He does not have to wait too long before notification is given by the person. The underlying principle is, "now that you are in a position of success or abundance, it doesn't mean that you will remain as you are: there will be times during which stress and need will arise. Therefore by giving and sharing, you are in a better position." Consequently, a person rarely gets upset by such minor "depredations," so long as notice after the fact is given. With regard to theft, there are two basic laws that can be applied. In most cases, the principal law is forgiveness, while compensation becomes the actual sanction if a particular law is violated after all the warnings. This is true in situations where mediation and consensus are reached by the parties concerned before making an appearance in a Village Court. Such cases are generally settled through forgiveness, while if the matter is to be raised in a court hearing, some form of compensation is generally worked out.

There is no strict law underlying leadership and control as far as to the extreme of applying immediate sanctions or force. There are recognised "big men" in the communities who carry out laws in attempting to restore peace and creating an environment of friendship.

The leadership succession in the whole of the Mambe Court area is achieved through individual effort. Some qualities of leadership involved wisdom, charity, defending other villages in tribal fights, knowledge of sorcery, and eloquence during social occasions.

Although this is not the case nowadays, formerly warfare and alliances would be initiated by recognised, influential men. Normally the big men or rather the big man of a particular village would make a move and then be followed by expert warriors into actual mobilization of the men. This particular practice seems to have died out over the last thirty years.

The underlying principle in customary law for housing and residence is quite flexible. No law forbids anybody from building his own style house. Apart from the residential style, the few exceptions include the women's monthly and birth period houses, or menstrual houses, which are normally smaller in size and have to be built a few kilometres away from the nearest community. There isn't much variation with residential location and residential status. People feel free to be on their own (moiety) piece of land, but the trend nowadays is very much flexible.

There is no clear-cut underlying principle in customary law for social obligations. However, if we are to specify particular social obligations, then surely there are some. For example, caring for the old and the sick people is up to any individual in that particular community. A normal pattern is for the members of the community to have respect or willingly show respect and have responsibility in as many ways as possible so that there is no sense of loneliness hidden amongst these types of people.

As far as other social obligations go, the main channel for rights and duties is applying for initiative. The younger people are often told what to do but not always. At times they are required to act independently, so that their behaviour can be assessed by members of that community and their capacity to act freely under given situations can be broadened.

In many instances, elderly people would be directors and organizers for a particular event which could be a joint session with another village or villages. In this regard, responsibility becomes jointly shared, particularly during feasting and marriage ceremonies. Women would form their groups while men form their own.

The underlying principle regarding premarital sex is that is dangerous to growth. This law is strongly upheld by the communities that make up this court area. It is strongly believed that people become weak, lazy and destructive to many of the societal rituals if they have sexual intercourse before marriage, especially if they are prominent figures in hunting, dancing, ceremonies, etc.

Again, a similar view is upheld for fornication, in fact, it is strictly prohibited. From the writer's observations, however, this particular principle has been gradually broken by many younger people nowadays, much more than it was some twenty or thirty years ago. Perhaps it may be due to certain frustrations and also as a result of social interactions between outside (town, other provinces, etc.) forces.

Generally from the writer's knowledge, there is no underlying principle in customary law dealing with incest, however the term of "biologically unintentional" was listed on the table simply to show that there is a biological element involved. Perhaps if there were a specific case, then surely a principle would be set down to rule it. Perhaps one of the common principles would be "shame" — within that family, by observers from within that community, and most likely those from outside as well.

With regard to other sexual offences, under western law, such as rape and homosexuality, it is always highly secretive between individuals involved. Although the writer does not have any specific cases on homosexuality, it is quite logical to think that where sexual freedoms are highly restricted between the opposite sexes, there can be acts of this nature in society if one is to release some of his many frustrations. Such acts would be highly secretive.

The underlying principle in customary law for family law has the following details. The commencing age for initiation is at puberty for both males and females. This particular stage of an individual's growth is very important in the sense that it is an historical event in a life cycle where one starts to become independent and marks the beginning of marriage preparation. Normally for the boys, the first stage of independence is for the boy to leave his parents' house and sleep in a single boys' house with other boys of his age group.

In bride wealth or bride price, the boy's relatives would normally pay a lot more than the girl's. While witnessing a marriage ceremony last December, it was evident that the boy's relatives who came along to assist both financially and in providing food came from almost all the villages within the Mambe Court area. A few extended relatives even came from outside the area. Similarly, the girl's supporters came from many different villages. The basic underlying principle in customary law under this title is for the boy's party to pay more, so that the fruits of the girl he marries will be towards his party and more importantly, that she will raise up children in his clan.

The exchange marriage system on a brother-sister basis is the most common feature of marriage throughout the Mambe Court area. In exchange marriages, parents of the boy and the girl come to some kind of agreement to place a trusteeship before the two people become a legally recognised couple or become legally prepared until such time as they are ready. The system is so strong that a family having only boys seriously considers adopting girls to at least match the number of boys. However, in most cases, a girl or a boy from within the extended family is eligible to be an exchange partner, and not necessarily from a nuclear family alone.

A general principle with regard to the dissolution of marriages is through the mediation method by parties concerned. From interviews carried out throughout the court area, there were hardly any case examples. This could be a result of the types of criteria involved in pre-marriage or premarital stages.

The underlying principles in customary law for adultery are "unlawful" and can be "compensatory". Persons violating their marital statuses in society are often labeled as low in status and sometimes "shame" becomes a stigma in their lives for some time. Some of the cases reported during the interview sessions were of this nature, but I never bothered jotting them down simply because the interviewees were boys because the men refused to talk about it.

The institution of polygamy is gradually vanishing as a result of public opinion. Prior to the coming of missionaries, polygamy played a significant part in society where succession to leadership involved competitive traditional politics. A man who marries more wives has many roles such as a warrior, witch doctor, peace maker and many more. He also possesses power within his own setting and outside as well if he is able to influence the behavior of many people.

The general underlying principle in the remarriage of widows, like dissolution and divorce, is through the method of involving relatives in a mediation process. The usual manner would be for a male widower to request for a particular female widow through the elderly men of his clan, whereupon negotiations would involve dialogue between the parties of both sides. The approvals can only be given where there are no stigmas attached and where every member in the mediation process agrees to whatever decision is reached.

The adoption principle includes fostering, orphanage, illegitimate children, guardianship and widows. Fostering occurs within a defined group while orphanage, guardianship and widows are with immediate relatives. However a woman with an illegitimate child has to bear her own responsibility in bringing up the child. Sometimes assistance can be given from other womenfolk within the lineage, but the general idea is to make that woman feel what it is to be like if she is not careful enough. Some widows can be solely independent and do not necessarily require assistance from relatives.

The underlying principles in customary law for menstruation are two-fold. Firstly it is regarded as unclean and secondly it is dangerous to growth and health. Women are strictly prohibited from any inhabited areas until their period is over. Similarly, they should not be in close proximity to domestic animals and should particularly avoid adult males. A mother who is having her monthly period is totally restricted from her house lest she endanger the physical and psychological growth of her children.

The basic function for sorcery and witchcraft is as a protective measure and also for the purpose of enforcing sanctions to restore justice or to maintain the status quo. The only common difference with the two terms are that the former is basically an art of destroying a person's life in any given form, so that a particular objective is achieved in the end, while the latter is an institution to treat diseases of the body and symptoms of diseases.

It is absolutely essential for a deceased person to be examined in order to identify possible causes of death before burial. It is also important that the body not be interred too quickly, so that relatives are able to come and pay tribute. A ceremony is held after the second week to end the mourning period and also more importantly to reconfirm the atmosphere in the house of the deceased.

The initiation occasion is totally compulsive for all youth to attend. A common practice is to have the male members introduced into the men's world of doing things while the female members are introduced to the women's spheres so that after graduation they are able to practice independence and self-help individually rather than relying on parents and other relatives.

The two common procedures in hunting are either individually or as a group. Individual hunting is more highly secretive than collective hunting, but both have to be initiated without women's knowledge. One common view hunters have is that if word leaks out to the women about a planned hunt, then surely the animals will escape from the planned hunting area.

THE IMPACT OF THE INTRODUCED LEGAL SYSTEM

The introduced legal system refers to the Local, District, National, Supreme and other court systems in Papua New Guinea which are based on foreign ideology or foreign concepts. How these courts have played a part in changing the attitudes of some of the people in Mambe Court area have been examined through interviews gathered during the research period.

From interviews held with the people and also from personal observations on Village Court operations generally, people displayed an unfavourable attitude towards the Village Court system. Some say that it is not very helpful and sympathetic, while other say that it is another court system just like the Local Court system which tries to punish people rather than providing an avenue for compromise, consultation, and mediation between conflicting parties. Therefore, they feel that there is no real need for the operation of a Village Court, and hold strong views that Local, District, National and Supreme Courts are much better and more preferable. One man even pointed out that in a Local Court, a neutral atmosphere makes the court procedure highly satisfactory while in a Village Court hearing one does not feel that open and free because he is surrounded by all sorts of pressures and the atmosphere does not look so friendly and easy.

Some men even pointed out that there was no choice given to the people to consider having a Village Court for the area. Others stated that it is gradually becoming expensive and creating social class between those that have the power of court officials and the majority of the people. When asked whether official qualifications made any difference between the Village Court and the higher courts, it was replied that they had no knowledge about that — all they were concerned about was the degree of neutrality and the atmosphere of an open environment from all sorts of pressures.

What is the present trend in the Village Court operation in Mambe court area? Again from the many views gathered during the interview sessions, it was strongly felt that the system tends to be in some isolation and not closely attached to the people. During court hearings, the Village Court officials would normally dress in a respectful manner with badges on their shirt collars. They would sit in an executive position just like the Local Court arrangement, rather than provide an atmosphere in a venue where the clients can easily express their problems and feelings flexibly.

CONCLUSION

The concluding paragraphs will feature firstly the relationship between the underlying principles and the impact of the introduced legal system, secondly the writer's critical opinion on this, and thirdly will give a short account on social aspects of life from the view of the people's changing attitudes.

Generally there has been a considerable amount of change between some of the underlying principles in customary law and that of the introduced or foreign concepts prior to the introduction of the Village Court system in Papua New Guinea. This is to say that some of the customary practices that were once effective are no longer effective because of the demand for a new or a more valuable alternative. The issuing of fines for punishment in Village Court rather than using other methods such as replacing stolen property is one example. Similarly if a woman has an illegitimate child nowadays, the case would go through careful examination and in most cases through higher courts such as the Children's Court for consideration of maintenance, while the underlying principle in customary law says that she has to be responsible for bringing up the child. However this does not imply that customary practices are gradually dying out, rather, the implication is that society grows and expands through many forms. The tendency to adopt to a new kind of situation or principle is desirable and necessary at the time. Therefore it is a little bit contradictory when trying to adopt a system such as the Village Court to help the people when the whole idea and the driving force in it comes from outside.

From the above viewpoint, the writer of this paper feels that the focus for improvement in customary law should be such that customary law reflects the fifth goal of, the national constitution — but more importantly as a foundation for other disciplines in regard to this goal.

A full programme on reorientation of the Village Court operation should be closely co-ordinated in the people's presence so that the changes in attitudes of people on any particular aspect can be made within a short period of time if there is to be any progress in the operation. This has to involve people in procedural planning generally for their own sake and not for any supervisory magistrate or anybody that is exerting force from outside. One obvious example is to reintroduce mediation, compensation and forgiveness as appropriate and desirable mediums and rather than imposing fines or granting punishment as an end result to those that break laws. Obviously this is not a very easy task, but through collective effort, something can be achieved.

The social aspects of life in this regard refer to many outside influences — innovations, ideas concerning new problems or knowledge which increase people's awareness — and generally how they interact with inside forces. One example is the Local Government Councillor for this area. Quite often the Councillor acts as a mediator or a middleman between conflicting parties and often the maximum penalty ordered is considerably lower than what the Village Court officials would order. Here the attitudes of the people can easily change to favouring the cheapest means and thus arguments can arise to condemn the toughest body which in this case would be the Village Court.

To conclude in a summary form, the effectiveness of the Village Court system rests heavily on the people's attitudes and wishes. Although considerable effort has been given by the people particularly to comply with system rules, a desirable approach would be to firstly inform the public through mutual respect and understanding so that they are aware about new types of changes. This would be preferable to conducting a two week course on the new arrangements of the court operation, attended only by the officials, or conducting something of such nature (in a village setting) and taught in a style similar to a teacher-student situation.

Therefore a recommendation would be for the Law Reform Commission to try out possible alternatives in Customary Law Development, to critically assess the present criteria that are being used (if there are any) for the Village Court system. The present nature of the system and its total scope are questionable and need reviewing if possible.

MIKAREW

MADANG PROVINCE

James Gissua

INTRODUCTION

One of the main aims of the Law Reform Commission in recent years has been to draw up a legal system which would be relevant to the people of Papua New Guinea. This has to be done in order that the laws governing the people can be understood by them and designed to serve their needs. The attempt reflects the inability of foreign legal systems to serve people of a different cultural heritage.

This report contains some general knowledge concerning the customs of the Mikarew people. The writer has no intention of compiling all written documents, which would be practically impossible. The views discussed in the report concentrate on causes and settlements of arguments or disputes. A general assessment of the operation of the Village Courts in the area will also be considered.

The aim of this research was to collect as many cases as possible (observed, memory cases, etc.) and then extract generalized statements of customary values, norms or principles of the area from these cases. The purpose was to gather information and send it to the Law Reform Commission in Waigani. The information sent to Waigani would then be used to help legislate a hopefully Papua New Guinea legal system.

AUTHORITY

There are "big men" at Mikarew as there are in many parts of PNG. Nearly every village in the area has its own big man. The big man is a leader in the village and exercises considerable power over his people. One of the main tasks of a big man is to organize, control and maintain the social, moral and physical needs of the people.

The big man, being the chief executive, has control over his officers. These officers include sorcerers, magicians, warriors and hunters. Under these officers are ordinary people; these men do whatever the big man expects. The political hierarchy is very loose. It is the big man who commands the people to make war, the sorcerer to practise sorcery, and the hunters to hunt.

There are two types of big men in the area. Each of them has a distinct role to play in the society. Because of the rapid social and economic innovations in the area, much of the powers the big man had have been taken away. The two types of big man are the **aruar dakosem** or warrior and the **amurisir dakosem** or mediator.

Aruar Dakosem (Warrior):

Literary, **aruar dakosem** means "aggressive table". It means it is at this table that the big man sits; it is from this table that he rules. This big man associates himself with vigour, aggressiveness and fury and is always on alert. He is a man of action and it is he that rules. He alone controls and co-ordinates activities in the village. He can tell the sorcerer to kill and the sorcerer kills, the magician to help the sick recover or cast evil spells and the magician obeys. Everyone listens to him.

The big man is a man of wealth and the people respect him for what he is. It used to be the custom that the first harvest from the new gardens be brought to the big man. Whenever people brought gifts, they brought their best because they respected him and feared him. Whoever disobeyed and went his own way was confronted with some trouble, whether it be natural disaster or something related to sorcery. This was a sign of their disobedience.

Amurisir Dakosem (Mediator):

The **amurisir dakosem** refers to the peace-keeping big man. **Amurisir dokosem** means "easy-going table" which in this regards describes the peace-building role of this big man. This type of big man is neither equal to the **aruar dakosem** nor has he power that overrides the decisions of the first big man.

The big man here is a mediator. For instance, if there were a fight between two groups, it is this big man's duty to see that peace is maintained. However, when the fight has reached an uncontrollable climax, the big man must not intervene. He can only act when the situation has cooled down. At this time, the big man acts as a go-between and negotiates peace between the two groups.

The symbol of peace includes a dry coconut and two handfuls of tobacco leaves. A serious event requires special preparation of selected bush herbs in which the juice is extracted and mixed with water. The solution is then put into coconut shells. Leaders from the two groups together extinguish burning firewood. This act is a sign of peace, with the fire representing hot passions and water cooling it off or extinguishing it. The presence of the big man makes the ceremony a more solemn act. Without his presence, the trouble is likely to continue. The big man **(amurisir dakosem)** has no control over sorcerers, magicians or anyone else. He is simply a peace-maker.

TRADITIONAL VALUABLES

The most valuable item in the area is called **atarim** — a whole range of dogs' teeth attached to traditionally made strings in rows forming a triangular shape. The value of the **atarim** depends very much on the size. The smallest one might be worth K10 and the biggest might be K100. The origins as to why the **atarim** has become so valuable are not fully known except that the **atarim** is being used as an important component for ceremonies.

Atarim can be paid as a compensation payment to relatives of a dead person by those who have been accused or were responsible for the death. In such situations, the relatives of the deceased can demand other goods besides the **atarim.** Other goods might include several pigs, several pig tusks, and some food from the garden. Before any price is paid, the respect and dignity of the deceased as seen by the society must be weighed carefully. The compensation price is paid according to the significance of the person. In any case, **atarim** must be paid in a case involving death.

The next traditional valuable is called **muter soguam.** This is a type of belt which is worn around the waist during ceremonies. It can range from ten to fifteen centimeters in width and varies in length. It is paid to the relatives of a person who has died some years previously. The ceremony, which can be referred to as an "appeasement ceremony", involves formal meetings of the relatives of the deceased and those who were regarded as being responsible for the death of the deceased. The **muter soguam** is included with other goods in forming a payment.

There are some other goods people value such as pigs, sago palms, land (owned by a clan), and yams, but these are not as valuable as the **atarim** and **muter soguam.** Owning several **atarim** and **muter soguam** means security, prestige and most importantly, a guarantee of life. However, these valuable items have lost their place in this society. Only village elders care about such things, and it seems that when these old people die, the newer generations will hardly have any knowledge of such things. If given a choice between K100 cash and an **atarim,** an elderly man would rather have the **atarim.**

DISPUTES

There are a whole range of arguments that the people involve themselves in every day. Through common knowledge, people try to avoid situations that would create ill-feelings amongst their fellow villagers. However, many times arguments arise because of some deliberate misconduct, or because someone is confronted with a difficult situation where an argument cannot be avoided. There are also occasions where someone does wrong specifically to provoke another person. Whatever the nature of argument, it can be between two people, two groups of people or between villages.

Arguments can erupt between husbands and wives over domestic animals and other family issues. People so often argue over sago palms, firewood, gardens, land, thefts, feasts, women and many more. Sometimes an argument may seem to be very small, as in a domestic dispute, but if not properly controlled, they can disturb the whole village and become everybody's business.

Many of the above mentioned incidents occur only occasionally. Those that occur frequently involve household problems and other minor matters. If, for example, a man finds out during the day that someone has stolen one of his watermelons, he would only complain to his wife or to whomever happened to pass by. He does not make a big fuss about it. He might learn later that one of his relatives took the watermelon, so that would be it. However, if someone digs into a mound of yams, then the owner becomes very angry. He would first go and see the big man (today, the Councillor) and ask for a meeting to be held immediately. The owner may have his own speculations as to the identity of the culprit, perhaps from past experiences. In most cases there is no real proof of whom to accuse. If a person is found guilty, then he or she either returns the yam he has stolen or pays back with a yam from his own garden. In most cases, those who steal are those who are referred to as **gueven** — which means the unfortunates who steal in order to survive. Yams are a prestige crop. One can give away other food crops, but to give a yam away is something that needs a bit more thinking.

The nature of an argument is very important. One must also be aware of the kinds of traditional methods used to solve disputes. The offering of a dry coconut and two handfuls of tobacco leaves served as a token of peace, in solving minor disputes. The **atarim** (dog teeth) signified peace between groups who are involved with more serious arguments. The big man (peacemaker) also played a very important part in maintaining peace in the village. Today, arguments are settled with money. One of the parties involved in an argument always sees that justice is accomplished through the transfer of money which has replaced the traditional **atarim** and **muter soguam** valuables.

Besides everyday domestic issues, there are those arguments which deserve special attention. These issues involve women, land, marriage, sago palms, gardens, trees and materials for housing purposes. For instance, at Abegini Village last December, Novi claimed a sago palm. Word reached Igeam of Ikemen village; and Igeam also had claimed that the sago palm was his. The two men were confused as to who was the rightful owner. Tensions arose, and neither of these two men worked the sago. After some time, a consensus was reached that each of the two men must take turns each time a sago palm is ready for harvesting. The agreement they reached will be honoured by their children and later passed down from generation to generation.

Sago palms are a source of wealth because people rely on sago as the main source of food during the long period of making new gardens. A person with a lot of sago palms is regarded as a wealthy man. Marriage arrangements are also affected by whether or not the boy has many sago palms. In this way, the girl or girls are usually encouraged by their parents to marry someone wealthy, i.e. who has sago palms, pigs, land and so forth.

Gardens are another issue. Gardens are the source of a large proportion of village food, and a threat to gardens angers owners. Normally pigs in the villages do not eat raw food, so many people do not bother to fence their gardens. If a pig is found eating food crops, the owner of the garden can spear it there or tell the owner about his or her pig. If the pig has destroyed half the garden, the owner can kill it because it would be wrong to keep such a pig which can cause a lot of problems for the owner. Many people complained to the Village Court about cows breaking through fences, eating up banana leaves and generally ruining the whole garden. Because of constant reports to Department of Primary Industry officers about cows, stricter measures have been taken. A cattle owner can be taken to the Local Court if his cows were found in a garden. DPI has also circulated prices of food grown in the gardens so that farmers can charge the cow owners accordingly.

The people have a tendency to regard village custom as something of the past. For example, it used to be the custom that when an argument was over, a party that has inflicted some physical injuries on another made an attempt to restore good relationships by offering a dry coconut and tobacco.

This was meant to be a sign of peace. Today it is the other way around: it is the party that received injuries which insists that the other party pay them. The payment always consists of money. Here one can see that those who demand payment take an active role. It used to be the other way previously, those who proved to be physically superior took the first step towards settling of the dispute. Paying money and restoring peace in the customary law are two different things.

Women:

Women are seen as potential co-workers of their men-folk, but more so as house-wives. Practical and informal education of women starts during their early years and continues right up until they get married. It is also over women that disputes arise. In the Mikarew society, premarital sex was never allowed. Adultery and fornication were never permitted. If a single girl had sexual relations with a single boy and no one knew about it, it would be their secret. But if there were some witnesses, or if someone suspected their activities, then an argument would develop. If it was discovered that an agreement was reached before the act, then the girl would be beaten up while the boy would be mocked and provoked by his parents and relatives. The father of the boy could beat up his son if pressured by relatives or out of shame. If it were found that the boy had persuaded the girl in the first place, then a fight would be likely to occur between the two parties. Usually under such circumstances, the boy's relatives and friends would remain passive knowing the guilt of the boy; filled with shame they could not retaliate.

On the other hand, when a single man has sexual relations with a married woman, and if they are found out, usually the woman is beaten up either by her husband or by her brother or first cousins. The actions of their sister brings a bad name and decreases their status in the society. The husband can either ask for compensation, which includes **atarim** and maybe a pig or two and several string bags of yams; or he can tell the woman (his wife) to move out from the house and return to her parents. The wife returns whenever the husband sends word for her to return.

Further still, if the husband finds that the wife has become pregnant from someone else, he again insists that she return to her parents to give birth. In other cases the woman gives birth and the child is given to the woman's parents. Sometimes the husband becomes so frustrated that he terminates the marriage completely. In some other cases, such a child is brought up only by the mother and the father refrains from any paternal dealings with him or her.

It used to be and still is the custom to avoid women during their menstrual periods. During this period, women are not allowed to prepare food or associate with others. They cannot handle food because it is believed that they are unclean and if they handled food or associated with others, it is likely that the sickness might spread. If a woman is found handling food for others during this period, she is reprimanded by older women and sometimes men. The same applies to women who have just had a baby. They have to live alone for a period of about six weeks before engaging in normal activities.

Domestic Problems:

Domestic problems refer to activities within the immediate family. Husbands argue with their wives over children, food, cleanliness in the house, and garden maintenance. It is the wife's duty to see that domestic animals are fed daily. Wives expect their husbands to provide housing and money, plant and make sago, hunt and do heavy work in the garden. It can be seen here that each of the two has a role to play. However, when one of them fails to perform his or her task, that is where trouble comes in.

Arguments within the family environment do not greatly affect the village society. Problems within the family are normal and there's nothing peculiar about them. But if the husband in the course of an argument beats up his wife badly, then his wife's relatives become angry. In such situations, the wife can flee to her parents until the husband sends for her. Usually, the husband would "buy" back his wife with an **atarim.** Her brothers and relatives should never fight with their in-law. It would be an insult if they did, and they would be filled with great shame. According to tradition, whenever such an incident occurs, a big feast is prepared to resolve their differences.

Land:

As in virtually all parts of PNG, land in this area is communally owned. Today land has come to be an area which attracts much attention; it has come to be a source of wealth and many serious disputes have taken and are still taking place. Land has come to be particularly important to the people now for two reasons: (1) the people have realized land shortages as the population grows each year; and (2) cash cropping and recently grazing have come to be the best sources of income and at the same time occupy a lot of land. Because of the above two reasons, natural borders happen to be areas greatly disputed. Here, the people rely on oral traditions and trace the stories back in order to prove their own claim against anyone who wishes to take their land.

It is obvious that no one member of a group can claim a piece of land for his own. This has been passed down through tradition. According to custom, members of a clan have their specific areas (within the land) to hunt, make traps or make gardens. These things were more important in traditional times than they are today. What is important now is to make those areas productive with cocoa and coconut trees. Clans with large areas of land attempt to raise cattle but those who have cows now complain that they do not have enough room to make their gardens. Thus there exist tensions within the clan. If people do not follow traditional rules, which is already the case, there will always be disputes. Whenever disputes arise, the big man is there to restore peace. Today it's the Councillor or the Komiti in the village that they see before the case is brought up to the Village Court, depending on the seriousness of the dispute.

Today, land means money. If a person has a lot of land, he has every opportunity to grow a lot of cocoa or coconut trees or other cash crops. Money has become more valuable than the **atarim, muter soguam,** or any other traditional valuables.

Marriage:

It used to be the custom that when a boy and a girl were born about the same time (within a few hours or days of one another) within the same village or in a nearby village, the parents and relatives arranged for the two to get married later. This tradition used to be very successful in the past but is not practised today.

When a boy is about ten years old, sometimes earlier, he is cautioned to live in the men's house or with his father. While living there, he is taught to obey certain rules which prepare him to undergo the initiation period. He must not take any food from any woman except his mother. It is the father or uncles of the boy who take the food to him. Sexual relations are strictly forbidden. Water consumption is very restricted as are baths. He gets a beating if he fails to observe one of these regulations. Acquiring of such training basically disciplines the boy for a successful marriage. A man becomes truly a man if he has undergone the initiation ceremony.

Today, however, marriages among the young people often revolve around education. For a girl in the village, an educated man means money, security, better clothes, and food, and so forth. Many girls wish to marry teachers, aid post orderlies, policemen and generally anyone who has had some formal education. Restrictions on premarital sex no longer exist and are completely ignored by today's generation. One elderly man said, "nau ol yangpela save man na meri save silip nabaut na marit olsem ol pik na dok", which means that everyone seems to play around with sex (which used to be regarded as something special); the marital act, which used to take place in a secret place, now seem to be done anywhere (like pigs and dogs).

Bride price is not very significant in this area. Formerly it used to be that some **erusim** (any traditional decorations used for ceremonies) were paid to the parents and uncles of the girl. A marriage follows such payments. Exchange of food and other goods such as betelnut, tobacco and money also takes place between the two groups. Today one hardly hears of bride prices in the area.

Today, marriages are somewhat less formal and often result from a couple taking up residence together. The break-up of such "trial marriages" can cause problems. For instance, suppose a girl lived with a boy (although not formally married) for about six months or a year and then left him. What normally happens in such a situation is that an informal investigation would take place and news would be spread to other villages. If the girl went away for some minor reason or just created some excuse to run away from the boy, people would put pressure on the parents and relatives of the girl to send their daughter back. In most cases she would return. If she refused, the parents of the boy would immediately request compensation. The compensation payment covers everything the boy spent on the girl while she was living with him. This form of payment has come to be commonly known as "baim lata" — which means the girl has failed to be true to the boy and his relatives and has brought shame to them. Failure to meet the compensation demands can arouse criticisms from relatives and friends of the boy in nearby villages. In a few cases, the girl's family may refuse to pay because they see the girl's case as legitimate. In most cases, however, payment is given immediately when requested.

CHANGE OF VALUES

It is evident in this area that traditional values (moral behaviours, respect for big men and elders, laws governing initiations and so forth) have lost their meaning. As mentioned above, the people no longer solve their differences with the big man (peace maker), nor is the traditional **atarim** or **muter soguam** significant anymore. Instead the people have substituted either the village councillor or a Village Court magistrate in the place of the big man, and money for the **atarim** or **muter soguam.**

Only a few people (especially the elderly) still value traditional ways of life. Many villagers (especially the youth) have a common belief that when the older people have died, traditions of the ancestors will be eliminated. For example, the art of relaying messages by beating a slit drum (garamut) is one of the most difficult tasks to learn. It is evident that instead of transmitting messages through the garamut, people will have to either write or walk distances to deliver messages.

The many changes are due largely to formal education (two-thirds of the people have attended at least at grade six); the impact of commercial activity (cash economy); church influence, and declining knowledge of ancestral ways even among the older people. Many of these elderly persons are people who have been working on plantations most of their younger days. There are a few trade stores and two Toyota land cruisers in the village. The average income for many people would be between K200 and K300 per annum.

VILLAGE COURTS

Village Courts provide a viable alternative to traditional conflict management techniques. The Village Court officials in the area consist of four magistrates (one is a senior magistrate), one peace officer and a clerk. This Court Division is known as Aruamu I (Aruamu is the name of the language spoken in the area).

At present all the magistrates are former Village Councillors. Only the senior magistrate is a traditional big man. The four magistrates also represent the four council areas. The senior magistrate's duty is to make sure that the Village Court system is running smoothly. He endorses whatever decision is made. He also makes sure that the books are kept in proper order and that monthly reports are sent to the District Officer at Bogia on time for inspection.

The three other magistrates take turns hearing court cases. In order to avoid suspicions of favouritism by the people about court decisions, it is usually arranged that whenever a case comes from Igos or Apovaiak or Iruari villages the magistrate from Abegini village hears the case; if the case involved people from Abegini then the magistrate from Korak or Arengen is there to listen to the case.

The peace officer is the most active member of the group. Whenever there is trouble, people will report the matter to the peace officer, otherwise he walks to the trouble area to investigate for himself. He reports to the senior magistrate or one of the other three magistrates about the trouble.

The clerk keeps the records of cases and writes up monthly reports that are then sent to the District Officer at Bogia. He has to be present at every court hearing and write up cases.

Courts are conducted fortnightly. The senior magistrate's residence is also the centre of the area so all court activities are carried out there. A magistrate, the peace officer, and the clerk are usually present to listen to the case. The peace officer is there to see that order is maintained all the time during the court proceedings. Occasionally people interfere with court proceedings and are fined.

One of the main purposes of Village Courts is to solve the people's problems acccording to the traditional customs of the area. Administrative officers have always referred land cases back to the Village Court because of the diversified involvement of customary laws.

There are generally three common types of punishments levied by Village Courts in the area:

1. The Court can ask the guilty person to pay a fine. The fine usually includes customary payments or cash money (the money goes to the Yawar Local Government Council).

2. With regards to minor cases, the court may decide to punish the guilty person by letting him do some physical work in the community for a given period of time (2-4 weeks). This includes doing tasks for the village and school community (cutting grass, building latrines, etc.) or digging drains and cutting grass along the main road or doing numerous other tasks at the Aid Post. Normally the Headmaster and Aid Post Orderly or Village Councillor will have a list of things they want done. The peace officer selects labourers (prisoners) to go to the different areas and supervises them when they are at work.

3. Those who commit criminal offences (adultery, assaults, use of dangerous weapons, etc.) are either jailed at Bogia or appear before the Local Court and many times end up at Beyon prison camp near Madang. Other times when the magistrates are confused, they refer the case to the Local Court without hearing it.

CONCLUSION

Many of our leaders (politicians, public servants, lawyers and community leaders) from time to time have expressed concern for a change in the present legal system. Many of them have emphasised that at present the laws do not serve the interests of the people of Papua New Guinea and remain foreign. In September 1979, Mrs. Nahau Rooney (former Minister for Justice) clearly stated in one of her letters to the Chief Justice concerning the Premdas case that the laws were not relevant to PNG. Towards the middle of 1979, a Special Committee with Tony Baias as Chairman was set up to review the Constitution. One of its major tasks was to seek opinions and advice from top public servants to villagers about the kinds of changes they would want to see instituted. The Law Reform Commission is engaged with research tasks so that relevant materials can be obtained. This was the basis for this research. The information gathered will help to direct lawyers and politicians to make laws that are favourable to PNG situations.

No doubt, one can see that there was a need for change in the national legal system. Research projects have been put into operation and are in the process of gathering information. Suggestions, criticisms, alternatives and amendments are coming in from all levels of people; from the elite class to the semi-elite and down to the grass-root level. We know that more than half of the people in PNG live in villages and only a small portion work in either urban or semi-urban areas. The question faced is who should have more influence on the law, the elite of the urban centres or the people in the villages.

The urban dwellers are a small group but are better educated; they have the knowledge of what has happened in other countries. The lawyers are within the elite group and claim to be the most suitable people to initiate any change and therefore it is only proper for them to work out the kind of legal system PNG should have. This small elite group is powerful in so far as influence over policies is concerned. After all it is the elected representatives (mostly elites) who have the final say in determining the law of PNG. Furthermore it is the elite who are in the position to collect information and can take the advantage to write their own ideas.

There are counter-arguments in support of the majority of the people (simple villagers) in considering changes to the national legal system; they are the ones who have had no formal education and will turn out to be the victims of the system. It is one of the principles of democracy to go by the majority; it is in the interest of the majority of people to determine their own legal system (meaning that no one faction dominates). It is the people that live in villages who really live the Melanesian way of life (if there is a Melanesian way) and not the elite in urban areas. Therefore, if there has to be change especially with the nation's legal system, then the major component must come from villagers.

The most important point is that the nation's legal system must be established to serve the 20th century people of Papua New Guinea. The law must do justice to the people of this land. Of course, certain universal principles must be observed in the light of humanity, e.g. the PNG legal system cannot justify "payback killing" as a genuine act. This leads one to become involved in morals and ethics. Our people have been influenced by the foreign missionaries and now have changed from their traditional gods to the Gof of Christians. However, the level of understanding of Christian beliefs by our people must be the same level that influences the legal system of PNG.

Since PNG culture is diverse, it would be very difficult to formulate a set of national laws that will satisfy every group of people. The legislators have a big task in front of them. They must get away from thinking on a regional basis: i.e. let none of them struggle to persuade others to believe that his customs are the best for the rest of PNG or that any one people's cultures should dominate, etc. The formulation of the national legal system must be rooted in the spirit of nationhood. Political differences from all levels of government must cease. That is why honest and loyal Papua New Guineans must be selected to formulate our laws.

There is also another problem. It is necessary to modify PNG's legal system now when the country is under going rapid changes. The number of people with formal education is increasing every year. By the year 2000, 75% or more of the population will have entered tertiary institutions or would have had some formal education; job opportunities will decline more and more and problems of urban drift will rise increasingly every year. PNG has modern electronic equipment, cars, machines, and already jet planes are flying in and out of the country every day.

The point is, are we trying to modify the legal system for the Papua New Guinea of yesterday, today and tomorrow. PNG has entered capitalism by keeping up with its latest trends.

The doctrines of capitalism are becoming more significant even to the normal villages. It seems that Western influence is accumulating in all corners of the country, and PNG today will not be the same tomorrow, likewise the law for PNG today will not be the same tomorrow.

AMELE

MADANG PROVINCE

Sanol Malaga

INTRODUCTION

This customary law research project was carried out in the Amele area of the Madang Province. The area lies some five kilometres southwest of Madang town and covers an area of approximately 200 square kilometres. Ohuru village, one of these Amele villages, was the base for research. The area is comprised of thirty-four villages and has a population of 7,162 which makes more than half the total population of the South Ambenob Census Division.[1] It is a patrilineal society. Ambenob is the name of the Local Government Council in the area. In July 1977, two Village Courts were established. The Amele Village Court No. 1 was established for people living in the northwestern part while Amele Village Court No. 2 is for the southeastern area.

The researcher has intentionally omitted various areas of customary law like marital age, procedure for entry into marriage, rules regarding domestic disputes, sorcery and many others. This is because these rules are hardly ever followed and are non-existent. They are non-existent in that the young men and women of Amele regard them as mere folk-tales. In other words, these customary laws are in a chaotic situation — there are breaches of them here and there, and no one actually knows what to do. The Village Courts also do not know how to go about tackling them. This is due to changes, as in many other areas, of so-called outside influences.

Those that will be discussed are traditional customary laws (or breaches of such laws) that are still recognized and are actually exercised. The compensations and procedures for settling disputes discussed in this report are also in a transitional period from payments using traditional items to the present modern form of money and goods. Most of these customary laws will be discussed briefly.

LAND OWNERSHIP

In the Amele area, land is exclusively owned by the clan or the traditional landholding group.[2] An individual, being a clan member, has every right to use the land. He can make gardens, hunt, or do other such things, but he cannot regard the land upon which he does these things to be solely his.

When disputes arise regarding land ownership, it is usually a clan versus another clan. Big men from neighbouring clans are invited by the clans in dispute to investigate into and determine the rightful owners. It is not easy arriving at a decision and the process is lengthy. The dispute may be heard and adjourned till the parties have gathered enough materials, witnesses to testify, etc. In cases where a clan member is in dispute with another, it is usually over a mere right to use a particular piece of land, belonging to the clan, and which the clan leader has allocated to one and the other may have ignored. In this sort of situation, the clan leader decides who is at fault. He may give his decision with the advice of other elderly clansmen.

There is no fixed remedy available to an injured party in land disputes. If one party groundlessly brings about the dispute in question, he is morally obliged to cook a pig plus other food in which everyone shares. The number of pigs depends on how many parties were involved in the dispute. If it resulted in engaging many other clans, the party may cook more than one pig. This restores peace and good relationships again. In general, however, as mentioned earlier, Amele customary law does not provide any remedy to the injured party and the other party is not liable to pay compensation.

PROPERTY OWNERSHIP

Natural Resources:[3]

The Ameles also regard natural resources like timber, sago leaves, vines, etc. as clan-owned. A clan member who wants to get these things must consult his fellow clansmen, although he can do it either before or after he gets the resources. The punishment for not consulting other clan members is a severe reprimand by the head of the clan. No further liability exists as far as the researcher knows.

Produce:

Garden produce, livestock, fruit trees (grown by the individual clan member) and such things are the property of the individual clan member. He is the sole owner of them, and therefore, as will be discussed later in cases of theft or personal property, he alone claims and benefits from compensation. Where conflicting situations arise regarding the ownership of a particular thing, all clan members are engaged in deciding who the rightful owner is. For instance, if there were a conflict between two clan members over a betelnut palm, witnesses would be brought to show that they were present during the time one of the parties planted it. Sometimes the Ameles inherit from a father who has died. In this case, the party seeks a witness who was present at the time his father planted the tree.

INHERITANCE

Land:

Inheritance of land in the Amele area is restricted within the clan. Thus, it is uncommon to have a dispute arising out of inheritance when both persons are within the clan. The only problem is when a child is adopted, but since the Amele customary law clearly states that an adopted child has equal rights to inheritance, this is usually easily solved. Males born within the clan are automatically "potential inheritors". However, there are exceptions to this general rule. A daughter may inherit the clan's land where: (1) there are no sons (2) the only son(s) is handicapped. Sons are "potential inheritors" until their father's death when they actually inherit. A child adopted by one of the clan members also has equal rights to inherit. A child adopted by one of the clan members also has equal rights to inheritance as a natural member, regardless of blood relationship.

Other Property:

With regard to inheritance of property other than land, for instance fruit trees, yams, wooden plates, clay pots, etc., the father has the discretion to decide whom to give a particular thing. In this case, potential inheritors may not only be his sons or daughters within his clan but also other people from other clans.

Usually, there is no conflict over inheritance when the father is alive. The problem arises when the father is dead. In this situation, the mother is relied upon for her decision. This is because she is recognized as the person "closest" to her husband who may have told her about his intention to distribute his property. The person who initiates a conflict over inheritance without good reasons is sometimes asked to give a pig to the injured party. This is not what an injured party would normally expect and it is up to the offender to do this. This is obviously to establish or restore good relationships again.

BRIDEPRICE

Brideprice is an area of Amele customary law which is in a transitional period regarding forms of payment, a transitional period from pigs, shells, and clay pots (generally a strict traditional payment) to modern money and other goods. The girl's relatives in the Amele area are the persons who determine how much a man has to pay as brideprice. Soon after the names of the parties intending to marry are announced, one of the chosen girl's relatives visits the man's relatives and lets them know the required amount of brideprice. Of course, it is not always as smooth as this. Parties sometimes elope to get married, which usually results in high payments of brideprice. Also, in ordinary situations, it is not uncommon for the girl's relatives to charge nothing. In any case, the man's relatives prepare for the payment, and at the date arranged, both groups meet and the man's relatives hand over the payments. The payments include pigs, clay pots, wooden plates, and many other items. There is usually no dispute involving brideprice payments except where the amount is thought to be unreasonably high. At present, this is one of the greatest problems in the area. It is not clear how such conflicts are or will be resolved.

BREACHES OF CUSTOMARY LAW

Adultery:

The Ameles regard adultery as a breach of customarylaw: it is very bad and shameful. In the past, death early always resulted.

To go about settling this matter, the adulterer must himself initiate the move. This he does, with the advice of his clansmen. It is uncommon to commit adultery within a clan. He admits the act to his elders and asks them to act as go-betweens with the injured party. When this is done, he gathers food, pigs, **awi-badom** (string bags sewed with dogs' teeth) and other compensatory items. His clansmen help to contribute. A date is arranged at which time he publicly apologises and shakes hands with the injured party. He hands over the compensatory items and social relationships are restored. If one does not do these things, he is branded a 'dog' forever[4] and will always live in fear of sorcery and shame.

Theft:

Stealing in the Amele is also a breach of customary law. However, the remedies available differ greatly according to the nature of the act, i.e. the value of the property stolen and the relationship between the guilty party and the injured party. If a person steals a big man's property, there would be a "great talk'' which would involve many people. On the other hand, if an ordinary man's property is stolen, it is considered a mere interpersonal dispute and could easily be settled.

If a person steals clan-owned property (for instance, sago leaves or timber) he is liable to pay compensation to the clan as a whole. This would mean that he would give more than one pig plus other goods. On the other hand, if he steals an individual clan member's property like garden-products, he may compensate by giving back a particular product or give a chicken to the injured party. This then restores the relationship.

CONCLUSION

Amele customary law is generally vanishing rapidly. The people, especially young men and women, seem to ignore their laws. For instance, when a young man wants to marry a woman, he does not tell his parents or relatives his intention or even seek their advice or consent. This is a common practice today. However, the two Village Courts in the area are doing their best to uphold the traditional methods of solving disputes. They can somewhat be described to be "resurrecting" Amele customary laws. The extent to which they may be able to revive customary law is still uncertain and doubtful.

FOOTNOTES

1. Census Office, Madang. Population figures as from November 1977. The researcher added the population of all Amele villages and subtracted it from the total South Ambenob Census Division population.

2. "Land" here includes water.

3. "Natural Resources" relates to resources an ordinary villager would recognize. It does not apply to such things as modern technology or science alone might recognize, such as gold, copper or silver.

4. In the Amele area, to be regarded as a 'dog' is very embarrasing, shameful and just unthinkable.

FINSCHHAFEN AREA

MOROBE PROVINCE

Jamoa Morriss

INTRODUCTION

Research was conducted in the Finschhafen Area of Morobe Province among the Yabem, Kale, Mape and Bukawa language groups. The total population of the area researched would be about 10,000. Information was gathered through observing Village Courts and through interviews, observing village meetings, hearing about memory cases, etc.

Despite the fact that these people speak four different languages, most of the customary laws are the same, and no separate categories can be distinguished. There is no distinction between civil and criminial liabilities as in western law. All disputes, conflicts or violations of established customary norms and rules are all seen as perpetrated against the person, and therefore the settlement procedure is more or less the same. In all cases, compensation payment or a settlement exchange of food and wealth is employed as a conflict-resolving mechanism. Settlement is reached when one party compensates the other or in cases of disputes and conflicts, when settlement exchange of wealth has been made. This indicates that the parties to the conflict or dispute have come to a meeting of minds or common dialogue that their dispute has been solved and is non-existent. Other reasons for compensation are that the wrongdoer realises his mistake and the payment is a conveyance of his apology to the injured party. An exchange also means re-establishment of good relationships between the parties and extinction of any shame that may have existed because of the dispute or conflict.

LAND

Individual ownership of land (meaning the soil) is unknown. The land is everybody's land. An individual may own what is on the land (i.e. betelnut, sago palms, etc.) but that does not mean that any of his clansmen cannot make a garden under those palms (see case 2515). When a dispute arises within a clan as to who should make a garden on a plot of land, everyone has a right to discuss the matter and the clan head has to give the judgement. Nowadays, this function is often taken by the Village Courts.

Transfer of ownership of land is also unknown. When one talks about a transfer, he means allocating a plot of land to someone for temporary usage. Permanent individual ownership is rare, although now that economic or commercial usage of land has been brought in, land ownership still remains communal but people begin to own plots of land in which they have their cash crops planted.

Any clan member has a right to do anything within his clan land, although he has a usage right only. He can hunt, fish, garden, cut palms or do anything on his clan land. However one doesn't have such a right if he is a stranger on another clan's land. If he hunts in another clan's land, and shoots a wild pig, he is guilty of tresspass. If he cuts wood or timber he is guilty of tresspass. Land boundaries are well-guarded and clearly marked. If you walk through another clan's land, you only have the right to pass through, not to touch anything on the land. Any cases of tresspass on land can be classified as stealing and are compensatable.

The societies in the region the research was conducted in, and in most other societies around Finschhafen, are patrilineally natured. Therefore every offspring automatically becomes a member of his or her father's clan. However the right to succeed the father remains with male members of the family. Every male has a right to succeed or inherit his father's property on the clan land. Whatever the father owns, such as sago palms, betelnut palms, or coconut palms has to be shared by all his male sons. However, there are certain exceptional cases:

1. If a man commits a crime which the clan feel is grossly wrong and is degrading to the reputation of the clan, such as committing adultery with his brother's wife, that man may be expelled from the clan. In this case, the expelled man loses all rights to inheriting his father's land. The reason is that it would always be a shameful and demoralising thing to have someone who has committed a crime against his clan remain with the clan members for whom he had no respect. After all, his father's land belongs to the clan for which he had no respect.

2. If a woman owned property on her father's clan land which she herself planted, then it remains her property even if she marries outside the clan. Her children will also have a right to use those properties or to own them, but they are not permitted to plant anymore.

3. In cases where a man dies and leaves a will concerning the sharing of his property, that will must be strictly observed. In this case, children of his daughters may sometimes have a right to inherit their grandfather's property. Where no will is left, then the sons are the rightful heirs.

4. In the case of a man who has no heir, then his eldest living brother takes charge of his property as a trustee and later distributes it amongst the relatives.

Where disputes arise between individuals within a clan, it is usually in relation to gardening plots (see case 2503). The clan head acts as a judge and, together with other clan elders, advises where one should end his plot and where the other should start. A problem within the clan is a clan matter. Today Village Courts replace clan heads and elders in performing this function.

Where there is a dispute between two clan groups (such as a boundary dispute), reliance is placed on oral history, traditional markers or past happenings to indicate where the boundary is or who should have land usage rights and who should not. The final settlement of all these disputes is an exchange feast to allow the disputants to mix and come to a common understanding to ensure peaceful livelihood in the future. In all cases there is always a middle-man, who acts as a mediator between both sides, usually a head or elder of another clan group.

ASSAULT

Assault usually doesn't occur unless there is a reason for it. If someone assaults another there is always a reason for it: provocation perhaps, or to settle a score or anything that makes one get angry so that he cannot control his temper. In cases of assault, the story of both parties is heard and weighed. Who was in the wrong, and what is the relationship between the parties? If there is an affinal relationship between the persons involved, the penalty imposed is usually greater than otherwise. In most cases, punishment is in the form of compensation.

DEFAMATION AND UNTRUE STATEMENTS

This is probably the main area in which conflicts usually arise as a result of day-to-day gossiping. Most disputes and conflicts today stem from untrue statements. When one party makes an untrue statement about another, and the other is upset about it or acts upon it, and later shows that the statements made were untrue, the maker is required to apologise to the injured party. In addition, he has to pay some compensation. Again the weight of punishment, particularly the amount of compensation, depends upon the lineal or affinal relationship between the parties. All affinal relationships are sacred, and the weight is usually heavy against the offender.

STEALING

This is normally done in relation to garden produce or household property. When one steals food from the garden or from a house, the owner has a right to reclaim the loss. Whatever method he uses is his business. But as stealing is a shameful thing, the villagers usually press for the return of the goods or property stolen. If a food crop has been stolen from a garden and is eaten up, then it becomes the responsibility of the thief to replace it or pay some compensation for it. Public shaming is also another punishment for stealing, and the only way to erase that shame is to hold an exchange feast with the offended to indicate to the public that you understand you have done wrong and you are sorry for it. If an exchange feast isn't held, then **silence** is used as a punishment against the offender. No-one will talk to or even smile at the person.

Stealing of communal clan-owned property happens in relation to tresspass on land or theft of ceremonial rites. That is if a stranger enters another clan's land and cuts down a palm tree, or fishes or hunts or does anything without informing the clan leaders, then it is classified as stealing. The implication is that your clansmen or ancestors were lazy and could not ensure that the things you got from another clan's land would be available on your own land. This sort of implication is very shameful for your clan. To remedy this it is your duty to compensate the offended clan but at the same time hold a feast for your own clansmen for the shame you have brought upon them. If you don't then you will be suspended from your clan and silence will be used against you until you have remedied it by holding the feast.

ADULTERY AND ILLEGITIMACY

Adultery is regarded as the most serious of sexual offences. In the olden days, both adulterers were killed to ensure that there would be no one around to remind people of the incident. There was no distinction between types of adultery: all cases were equally serious.

When someone commits adultery with a clan brother's wife today, the case would result in divorce for the woman and expulsion from the clan for the brother. The woman loses all custody of her children. It is a shame for her clan, so her clan has to compensate her former husband for the wrong their woman did to him. The brother is also expelled from his clan because he had no respect for his brother whom he offended, so customarily he doesn't deserve to be within the clan. He loses all his land rights and others also. He also has to remove himself from the presence of his clansmen. When this happens, the brother then moves to his wife's clan or his mother's clan area. After several years, if the clan leaders of the new clan are happy with him, they might give him clan membership and thus all clan rights of that clan, but for his clan he is finished. However, even this practise had become rather rare today, and is more an ideal than a real rule. An offender may only get a suspension pending a pig or settlement feast for his brother and clansmen.

Illegitimacy also is seen as an offence in the societies within the research site and around the Finschhafen area. The reason is that premarital sexual relationships are forbidden, and when an unmarried girl or woman conceives, it indicates that she has broken the norm. Furthermore, it brings great shame on her parents and clan group, because it implies that she is a tramp. When this happens the pregnant woman goes into hiding and may never find a husband, as a punishment for her breaking of the norm.

BRIDE PRICE

Bride price payment is a practice of the people of the research site. When a couple marries, it is expected that the husband's family and clan members will pay some form of bride price to the woman's family. The reason is that the woman will bear children who will be members of that clan and become workmen of that clan. At the same time it is expected by the man's parents that their son's wife will make her services available to them. If bride price is not immediately paid, then when the parents of the woman demand it, it should be paid. If it isn't paid the woman may refuse to make her services available to her husband's parents and family group. In addition, her clan may advise her not to allow herself to bear them a child. If she already has had a child, then that child is sent to the woman's brothers to be looked after. A case may arise where bride price has been paid but later the wife divorces her husband for some reason or another. The man's clan have all customary rights to reclaim the compensation (see cases 2505 and 2516 as typical examples).

LOU ISLAND

MANUS PROVINCE

Fraser Pitpit

INTRODUCTION

Before I proceed, I would like to make clear the location of my research. This paper concentrates on the customs of the four villages on Lou Island in the Manus Province: Rei, Lako, Baon and Solang. Most of the customs and principles discussed would be similar throughout the south coast islands of Manus Province, such as Baluan and Pam.

LAND OWNERSHIP

With regard to the subject of customary ownership of land, I think it is relevant that I should describe the basic social units on Lou Island.

1. Immediate Family: This unit extends to any of the members of a marriage, i.e. parent(s) and their children.

2. Lineage: The unit extends to any of the members who originated from the same male founder or male of the family.

3. Clan: This is the kinship unit wherein activities such as trading, fighting, etc., are accomplished jointly. It can be defined as a sub-tribe.

4. Tribe: A tribe is the inclusion of all units, and is responsible for the success of its members, i.e., the members of families, lineages, and clans in that tribe. I must make clear that the tribe as a whole cannot settle conflicts among families unless the conflict involves another person from another tribe.

Land ownership corresponds with the social units described above. In other words, consider the Mellie tribe on Lou Island, with about 100 members. There will be an area of land owned by the Mellie. This land is divided amongst clan groups of the Mellie, and further subdivided into lineage holdings. Even these lineage holdings are further subdivided into family group lands.

General rules regarding land ownership:

1. Ownership through birth: Land ownership cannot be passed on to an individual unless he was born in the family. Such an individual is automatically accepted and recognised as a family member, and therefore his rights to usage of family land are secure.

2. Adoption: In cases where an individual is adopted into another family, he automatically loses his usage rights to the land of his original family and is recognised as a member of the new family. The rights to the ownership of the new family land is recognised by the community.

3. Male ownership of land: Mostly, ownership of land passes through the father's side. Females very rarely own land or become landowners. Since females marry outside the immediately family unit, their rights to the usage of land are not so much recognised. However, there are cases whereby females have become landowners. Females can become landowners in cases where the land has been presented to her by her family as a gift, where it is given to her as brideprice **(tolva),** or where she is the only member of the family.

Ownership of land can be transferred outside the immediate family unit:

1. In cases where an outsider buries a landowner. This is often done in cases where the dying man has no other relatives, or in cases where the close relatives of the dying man do not treat him as he desires, then before his death, he makes a verbal will that his land will pass to so-and-so if they bury his body. This practice is a sort of contractual arrangement.

2. In cases where land has been obtained as a good-will sign or as a gift. For instance, if my father was a friend of your father he might give you a piece of land to work on and support your family.

In cases where someone is using a piece of land owned by another, the user is not allowed to plant permanent cash crops. In cases where the user planted permanent fruit trees, the customary owner of the land will own the fruit trees.

Land Problems:

Long ago , land conflicts were not as common as today. Two factors which contribute to current problems are population increases and cash cropping. Population during the recent years has rapidly increased. This is due mainly to the work of modern medicines and science. With more lives saved, land is becoming less available all the time, therefore people are making false claims on land (see case 1802). Cash cropping is another of the factors which has contributed to the problem of land conflict. Although land was valuable to the people in the past, it wasn't until the introduction of cash crops such as copra and cocoa that conflict has become common. During the past, communal work was common. Recently, communal work has become a virtually nonexistent matter. People are tied up with their own business and no one cares for another. I blame cash cropping for such an attitude. Another thing which I blame for this attitude is the introduction of Village Courts. I don't agree with the Village Court system because of my personal view of the system as it operates in my area. Of course, my view is subject to change through explanation and in the interest of the public. My basic argument is that, before the introduction of such a thing, the people responsible for the system should have foreseen that such a system would spoil or destroy communal responsibility. It has now gone beyond weakening collective responsibility. In order to create peace, it is doing just the contrary. It is in a way slowing down development. For example, if two people are involved in a conflict in the Village Court, and one is found guilty and fined, the relatives of that person will not want to help his opponent or his opponent's family with anything.

MARRIAGE

There are actually three types of marriages now in existence on Lou Island.

1. Legally-bound marriage, i.e. where the spouses simply sign a registration form in front of a magistrate.

2. Church marriage, where a marriage is performed by a church official.

3. Customary marriage, where a marriage goes through customary marriage procedures.

According to my findings, the second method is more commonly used since Independence. However, I have decided to discuss the third form of marriage in keeping with the purpose of this report.

Customary Marriage:

With regard to the kind of customary ceremonies used, I have very little to say since customary ceremonies are no longer closely followed. Procedures of customary marriage are usually adopted to modern conditions in one way or another, and to a certain degree blend with all forms of marriages I have mentioned above. For example, in all three marriage methods, consent of uncles must be obtained, or, in naming of children, usually names are names from the mother's side.

The spouse (actually the wife) is chosen by parents or uncles of the man. It is very important that persons other than natural parents be included in choosing the spouse. This is because of the principle of collective responsibility, or to put it straight, it is called kinsmen responsibility.

Right of choice on the part of the man is very limited by the great pressure coming from both sides, i.e., from the mother's side and the father's side. The mother's side will press the man to marry someone from their side, while the father's side will at the same time press the man to marry someone from their side. This is simply for the beneficial reasons. If your choice is to marry someone from your mother's side, they would benefit. However, the father's side would also benefit, since you have a responsibility to both the mother's and the father's side. When the spouse (female) has been chosen, it is the duty of the male's family to go secretly to the female's parents, usually in the night, and ask the girl's parents. This process is known as **rongrong** which means listening or asking.

It is a very serious sin if two closely related persons have sexual intercourse or get married. It is a great sin because it is thought to result in disfigured children and also because a generally bad stigma is attached to such behaviour. If a person commits such a sin he may lose some of his rights and privileges, e.g. rights to land and privileges of a member of a particular family.

The system of customary marriage on Lou Island did not in the past emphasise bride price except as a sort of exchange. Usually, during the marriage ceremonies, it is the wife's side which prepares the food for the man's side to eat. Only raw food is carried away by the man's side, and it is this food which has to be paid for. Therefore I see the system as an exchange rather than bride price payment. In cases where a husband divorces his wife there is no rule of custom which provides for the return of the "bride price". I must thus say that in the customary law of Lou Island there is no such thing as real bride price.

Marital Disputes:

There are several problems and disputes which arise between married people. Two of the most common causes for general sorts of domestic disputes are:

1. Sexual intercourse: In cases where a spouse, say the wife, refuses to have sexual intercourse, the dispute will be settled between the spouses. Since it is a private matter, the public have no right to hear the case. If it cannot be settled, the husband's only option is to break up the marriage and send the girl back to her parents.

2. Adultery: This is another case which has to be settled between the spouses on the first attempt. However, if it fails, the matter may be brought before the village elders, and the chief. This case has two options today, either it is brought before the church committee or before the Village Courts.

The remedy or penalty with regard to church settlement of disputes will be suspension for a period of time, i.e., three months or so before attending church services or playing any church roles.

Divorce in a formal sense does not exist on Lou Island. Couples merely split up. Some of the reasons causing couples to separate are listed below:

1. Adultery: Where one of the spouses has been unfaithful to his/her partner. It must be made clear that male adultery is not considered as serious as a married woman's adultery. Often it is the husband who divorces his wife, because wives don't initiate divorce. They simply return to their fathers.

2. Sexual intercourse: Where the wife usually refuses to have sexual intercourse regularly or when the husband wants it without good reasons.

3. Neglect of duties: Where a wife refuses to cook for her husband, or neglects to make gardens, or is lazy.

4. Abortion: Since the aim of marriage is to have children, if the wife commits abortion she can be divorced.

GENERAL WRONGS

Stealing:

Stealing is a wrong which is sometimes difficult to define as stealing. The strict definition as given in the criminal code cannot be applied successfully in most cases on Lou Island because stealing is viewed in two different ways. An act of stealing in the customary sense involves an enemy or a person who is not related to the complainant one way or another. If a man takes another man's canoe to go fishing, without his consent, this could be stealing if the men are not related. On the other hand, if one is related to the other, there can never be said to have been a case of stealing. This also applies in cases where food is harvested without the garden owner's knowledge. For example, one person might harvest the bunch of bananas without first obtaining the owner's consent if they are related in one way or the other. In cases where an individual intends to deprive another of his canoe or other property, he can suffer from various forms of punishments including being shamed in public or having to make another canoe to replace the one he stole and damaged. In cases where a person steals coconuts, bananas, etc., the banana sucker or coconut husk will be placed in front of the house of whomever stole the items. This is intended to shame the person involved.

Defamation or cursing:

Defamation occurs mostly in the form of gossip. Defamation in general is not allowed. Defamation between husband and wife is not considered as serious as when it is repeated by the third party. Cases of defamation are usually settled between the parties involved. If no solution is reached, the matter will be brought before the village elders. The village elders are the last resorts. This is where compensation is arranged. In cases where cursing occurs, the same procedures are followed. In both cases, public apology is necessary.

Sex Offences:

Incest is rarely committed, however there have been a few cases where incest has been alleged. In cases where incest has been committed within the immediate family, the punishment is usually very heavy. In some cases, the parties involved leave the family and go their separate ways. Before they leave they are caned publicly and cursed. The degree of the punishment however depends on the degree of relationship.

In cases where sex is practiced before marriage, prohibition is not really emphasised. It depends on the extent of freedom given by the parents. Since most parents want their children to get married, some degree of prohibition is exercised, but all in all, premarital sex is practised.

NEW HANOVER

NEW IRELAND PROVINCE

Soiat Williams

INTRODUCTION

Over the University Christmas vacation period from the 19th November to the 19th February 1980, and subsequently in 1981, the Law Reform Commission recruited one or two students from each of the provinces in Papua New Guinea to research the customary laws which existed and were practiced in his or her area. The aim of the research, as stated in the Commission's handout, was that when the researchers went out to their research area, they should report any conflict cases, and most importantly take note of the principles being used by the elders or other persons settling the disputes. It was hoped that these findings about principles of customary law would provide some relevant information for the Commission to formulate a legal system for Papua New Guinea based upon these Melanesian principles.

Before proceeding to the body of this report, it is my intention to describe the general structure of the report. The first part will be confined to a general overview of the geography and people of New Hanover, followed by a discussion of the actual location of the area I covered in this research. The second part, and I suppose the skeleton of this report, will describe the principles and laws expressed in my cases. I will add to the second part some of the past customary principles and laws used by our forefathers which are not commonly practiced by the present generation. The final part of this report will be confined to topics such as land tenure, principles of inheritance, and principles of ownership.

One might wonder why I need to have a section on the summary of principles and another on past customary principles. Research findings indicate cases of the same nature where principles vary. To illustrate, in the past, if I were related to some clansman, it was not necessary for me to go and ask if I wanted to climb his betelnut tree. What I would have done would be to climb it and if I did not see him around, I may have informed him of what happened. However this is not the case today. There is a principle protecting individual's rights to their properties, so if I want to climb my relative's betelnut nowadays I have to seek his permission beforehand.

I suppose such variations in some of the customary practices and customary principles have come about because of the rapid impact of political, economic and social changes in traditional society. One of the social factors that could be said to be responsible for such a decline in traditional practices is that the present and upcoming generation aren't eager to maintain such practices and do not possess any knowledge of them.

FIELD SITE

Geographically, Hew Hanover (Lovongai) lies at 2°3′ S and 150°15′ E. The island is 30 miles long and 21 miles wide. Like the islands lying along the eastern coast of New Ireland, New Hanover is mountainous and volcanic in origin. The island is transversed by the Tirptz range throughout its length. The vegetation of New Hanover is tropical rainforest, while its coastline is fringed with mangroves throughout. On the northern coast there are chains of islands lying parallel to the coastline. This chain of islands supports much marine life, as clearly indicated by the present intensive fishing activity by Tropical Fisheries Pty. there. New Hanover is separated from Kavieng by the Byron Strait.

The people of New Hanover are like their Melanesian brothers of New Ireland. Their mother tongue is **Tungak** which is spoken throughout the island with minor variation in pronunciation. The present population ranges from 10,000-12,000 people. During World War II New Hanover people were described by Americans as "intelligent and sophisticated" with which I totally agree. Like many Papua New Guineans having experienced social change, the Lovongai people have modified their lifestyle towards a Western style of living.

As I mentioned earlier, the research was carried out in New Hanover. I was based on Mamirum Village. Occasionally I would travel around the island to gather comparative data. If I did stay overnight I would start off a discussion of such topics as land tenure, principles of inheritance, etc. The areas I could cover were limited due to transport difficulties. I was forced to walk or take a canoe, although sometimes I got a ride on the mission boat of the parish.

Table 8.1 below shows the villages covered in the research (group 1) and the villages visited for comparative data (group 2). Population figures refer only to people over the age of 18.

Table 8.1

VILLAGES VISITED DURING RESEARCH

GROUP 1

Village	Approximate adult population
Kung	50
Tunnung	10
Tabut	50
Meterankasing	35
Naitab	25
Puas	55
Ungalik	100
Metemin	10
Patpatigan	30
Lukus	20

GROUP 2

Village	Approximate adult population
Taskul	300
Lovongai	200
Patipai	100

PRINCIPLES OF CUSTOMARY LAW: SUMMARY

Traditional Leaders:

Today, in the village that I covered in the research, the appointment of village leaders is the same. They are there to serve their fellow villagers, to act as judges of cases, and to lead their clans in social gatherings and other activities.

In some villages, the village leader does not hear any case alone but rather chooses some elderly, well-respected villagers of good character to form a panel which will be responsible for executing the role as judges. Ungalik Village has a set-up like this. In the areas in which I did my research, village elders do not receive any form of payment for their work. If villagers have any case that they want to solve, they inform the village leader, who decides the date, and where the case will be heard. One of the most important principles noted in this research is that, in the process where the leaders have to hand down their decision on any case, they will always consider the family relationship of the parties involved in the case.

Personal Property:

Amongst the cases I worked on, the principle of ownership revealed is that any property remains the property of the owner plus his or her family. If any person other than the family of the owner is found, say, going into a house without the consent of the rightful owner, the person is liable to pay compensation for such. This principle does not apply to individually owned property alone, but could be applicable to property owned by the village or clan. If any person from a different village or clan is found using any property belonging to another village or clan, that person, or village or clan, should compensate for the action. In other words, what is emphasised here is that items not belonging to a person must be left alone unless the rightful owner's permission for use is secured beforehand.

Sexual Intercourse:

In this society, sexual intercourse is a serious offence for people outside of marriage. This offence applies to church marriages, government and traditional marriages alike. It is strictly enforced that any sexual relationship must be kept a secret. If two single persons were involved in sexual activity and are found responsible for revealing their affair they would make compensation payments in the following manner. First, both would pay equal amounts to their partner's relatives. If J., a male, had an affair with K., a female, J. would make a payment to K.'s relatives and K. would in response pay J.'s relatives. If J. were married and K. were single, the normal practise today is that J. would pay K.'s relatives an amount equal to the payment which K. would pay to J.'s wife. J. would still have to pay some money to his own wife for having sexual intercourse with K. If both were married, then both would have to pay their wife or husband equal amounts of money for having sexual intercourse.

Family Cases:

In any family cases, no matter what the nature of the problem is, it is a principle that the family must attempt to solve it first. We have such principles to maintain our respect for that particular family, for family security and family identity in general. However, where the first attempt has failed, and it is of such a nature as to affect the relatives of the married couple, then external help can be sought either through the village leaders or relatives of both people involved. It is a strong principle that under no circumstances should people make any attempt to resort to violence in dealing with their in-laws.

Respect and Social Conscience:

Respect in society must be maintained among all ages and all walks of life. The principle of brotherhood should be kept by all families when they live in their villages as attested to by the practice of serving visitors with food free of charge and assisting them whenever they need it. It may be surprising, but it is a common practice in New Hanover that when total strangers come on our shores, people have to hurry up to prepare some food and make the visitors comfortable. The people I worked with say that this practice brings the people peace, harmony and the greatest satisfaction. Given this stress on social harmony and respect, when one member of the community is offended, the person responsible is expected to compensate for such irresponsible action.

Marriage:

I thought of discussing this topic under the category of "family", but I have decided to put it separately because of certain aspects relating to the choice of marriage partner. In traditional society, parents are responsible for choosing whomever their sons and daughters will marry. However today this is not the case, and any male or female when he or she is old enough to get married can choose their own partner for life. Society in the past regarded marriage as a means of increasing the population of the clan and a means of uniting other clans with it. In those days, one marriage practise was that, before the actual ceremony of uniting the male and female, the girl would go to the boy's relatives' home and live there for approximately two months. This period could be regarded as a trial period for the girl to prove to the boy's relatives that she would make a good wife. When the woman proved her ability to be a wife, then the ceremony would take place and the clans of both partners would participate in the ceremony. Today, sexual intercourse amongst single boys and girls in the village is a licence to marry.

PRINCIPLES OF CUSTOMARY LAW: DISCUSSION

Since the legal principles of the traditional society of these people are not written, they can only be recognised when someone within the village is affected physically or mentally. In the past there was a tradition of punishing people who were engaged in rape, sorcery, breaking other traditional laws, theft of other people's property (e.g. sago or garden produce), adultery, mistreatment of women, sexual rivalries, etc., with death.

I suppose such a severe penalty restricted people from committing such offences. In fact, when I asked some of the elders, they remarked that in the past people lived a much happier life because of the fear of death. For domestic cases of family affairs it was totally left to each family to solve its own problems with assistance from the elders and relatives where necessary.

Extended family ties within the society form the fundamental basis of any clan. If the family relationship is not firm, there is a possibility of losing land or other communally-owned properties because of arguments over inherited property. Since the society has realised this, it has ensured that the principles of brotherhood and solidarity within the family be emphasized. If there is any dispute within this group, it must quickly be settled.

Traditional exchange as a means of settling a dispute is shown in case 2104. Exchange of food and traditional money (cash money may be used as a substitute) was used to resolve such differences. However, such exchanges do not always end a dispute. One of the indicators of ill feelings is for one family to put more food out during an exchange, thus creating an imbalance and signaling their counterparts that they are still angry. During such an exchange ceremony, both parties may shake hands, but the village elder will remind the other family that they have to repay more to equalize the amount of food put out by the other family. The only time such a dispute is fully settled is when both sides have made an equal exchange.

Inheritance and Land Ownership:

Today, land is passed on only through inheritance. However, there were three ways through which the ancestors of today's land owners acquired land:

1. Through one clan fighting another clan with the winner occupying the land.

2. Through original occupancy of previously unused land.

3. Through going to an undiscovered piece of land and making a mark by planting food plants (e.g. sago) and then returning back to the village. People who later go there and settle there will be told to stay away from that particular land which has already been marked.

Two general types of inheritance are followed in this society: matrilineal and patrilineal. Matrilineal inheritance is based upon female ancestry. With regard to land inheritance, male children own any property of their mother's family. We have the same land usage rights as our mother's brothers and sisters. However, when male children get married and have children, those children have no right over the land which is owned by their grandmother's family. However, this is not the case for female children's children. They will all have the right to own the land and use it just like their mothers.

Patrilineal inheritance (from father to son) is occasionally practiced in this society. For example, if I want my children to have the same rights as my sister's children on our land, I have to arrange with my mother's brothers and sisters and with my own sister that I wish to do such a thing. If they agree, I will have to arrange a buying ceremony with feasting and dancing during which it will be announced publicly that my mother's group has extended rights to ownership to my children (but **not** to my children's children).

CONCLUSION

The principles and laws discussed in this report show the changing nature of customary law. While these people are aware of the fact that they no longer practise some of the traditional ways of their ancestors, they have maintained some of the basic principles of peacefully maintaining their society. Of all the principles and laws discussed here, they claim that the principle of brotherhood to all no matter what creed or race is the most important one. There is a strong value placed on maintaining peace and social harmony. Under this principle, every family has the responsibility to see that their children live as the society expects them to live. It is their responsibility to see that respect for others is maintained and any form of assistance provided to any person within their reach. Violations of these principles today are regarded as a disgrace. This strong sense of social responsibility has led to a relatively peaceful society today. It is questionable, however, whether these principles can be maintained as time goes on.

NAMATANAI DISTRICT

NEW IRELAND PROVINCE

Sios Naibuka

INTRODUCTION

My research on certain principles of customary law was conducted in three Village Court areas in the Namatanai district of the New Ireland Province. These are as follows:

1. **Sursurunga-Tangalamet:** The Sursurunga area, as it is commonly called, has an approximate population of 3,054 living in about twenty villages south of Namatanai town, from Balai Village to Muliama Village. In this area I interviewed a number of elders, but special mention goes to Village Court Magistrates Todiot Amen, Lias Kiaprimen, Eli Durirong and Maikeli Kiapsiner.

2. **East Patpatar:** The East Patpatar area has an approximate population of 3,612 living in about seventeen villages beginning at Pire Village to the north of Namatanai town and bordering at KuduKudu Village to the south. Special mention goes to the village elders and Village Court Magistrates Sisi Malkom, Sangin Pili, Petrus Tade, Raphael Patan and Kiapnar (of Rativis Village.)

3. **West Patpatar:** The West Patpatar area is to the west coast of the East Patpatar area. This area has a population of 3,145 living in about sixteen villages from Palabong Village in the south to Labur Village in the north. In this area, which I feel is my own area, I did my own observations with few interviews. However, on some occasions I was helped along by some people. Special mention goes to my uncle, Sioni Lala Naibuka (the oldest surviving person in our community, born 1880), and my father, Sios Tabunamangin Naibuka who spent considerable time assisting me in my research. Since they are more familiar with the whole of

the Namatanai and the islands, their assistance was very much appreciated as it was very helpful.

General speaking, my people live very much the same easy-going life-style as our great-grandparents, even though we have been in contact with white influence for well over a hundred years. We believe we have always lived in these lands and I have no knowledge of any myth or legend that may explain our possible originations. Social organisation in the Namatanai district, as the whole of New Ireland, is matrilineally based. Land rights and descents, etc., are matrilineally traced, linking the children with the mother's kinship group. Because of this, customs and customary law rules and principles are more or less the same all over New Ireland. I believe that there is no distinction between civil and criminal law(s), because what is right is right and what is wrong is wrong. However, there is a distinction between a serious wrong and a minor wrong. These are related to the degree of relationship between parties to the dispute. Minor disputes or conflicts are limited in scope and usually involve members of the same family, clan or moiety. Major or serious disputes involve members of different families and clans and separate moieties. Table 9.1 provides an outline of substantive law categories in the Namatanai area.

Table 9.1

SUBSTANTIVE LAW OUTLINE

INTER-PERSONAL CONFLICTS/DISPUTES

1. domestic arguments (husband and wife, etc.)
2. disputes over women/men (over adultery, mistreatment, etc.)
3. disputes over wealth/belongings, etc.
4. thievery of another person's property.

INTER-CLAN/FAMILY DISPUTES OR CONFLICTS

1. land matters (ownership, boundary, etc.)
2. succession or inheritance.
3. wealth credit (not repaid).
4. sorcery.
5. thievery of another clan's or family's property.

BREACHES OF CUSTOMARY LAW

1. non-performance of customary obligations (e.g. family obligations; funeral feasts).

2. thievery.

3. trespass (burying in another clan's cemetery, etc.; or trespassing on another clan's land).

LAND

Land to us is very special. Our connection with the land is somewhat spiritual and natural. It is our most valuable asset; everyone owns land, uses it, eats out of it, and is buried in it upon death. Therefore, we have a very intimate relationship with the land. This relationship is neither individualistic nor really materialistic. We have an interest in anything found on or associated with the land. Land to us means survival. It is our life.

Land Ownership:

A clan owns the land. Each clan has various rights to and interest in its land, and each has its own spiritual figures, spirits, cemetery, and magic or sorcery powers associated with their land. Other clans recognise and respect these interests as well as the area of land belonging to the particular clan.

Land Use and Allocation:

As the land is owned by the clan, everything found on or growing on the land is used by and belongs to every clan member. However, individual members may have exclusive rights to crops such as coconut trees (traditionally used for eating and more importantly for feasts and feeding to pigs, but now for copra), garden and food crops, breadfruit and nut trees and sometimes betelnut trees. Still, every clan member and relatives can use these crops. That is, there is the overriding principle of the clan owning the land and everything found or growing on the land.

"Exclusive rights" may be strictly exercised during allocation of land. Active clan elders, especially an uncle or an active female elder, have the exclusive right to allocate or "give" to a clan member his crops or "portion of the clan's land". Upon the death of such a recipient strictly speaking, his crops or "portion of the clan's land" automatically goes back to the clan. But, in reality, it often goes to whomever he or she has named, usually **ira hinsakana,** meaning and implying his or her family members or close relatives.

There are even cases of a man "giving" or allocating his crops (especially coconuts and garden crops) or his "portion of land" (the area within his clan's land where his crops are located) to his children. This is rare in a matrilineal society. In such situations, the children have access to the use of the land and the crops growing on it, or planted by their father, but the land is still and will always remain the property of the father's clan. The father's clan can reclaim the land, especially if the children have not performed or contributed to the father's funeral feast, or if the children have not performed some obligation required by custom. But the land cannot pass from the father's children to their children. After the death of the father's children, the land goes back to the original land-owning clan.

Land Succession:

Succession to land use, and thus allocation, passes to someone who may have been named by the deceased. Otherwise, it passes to the person (male or female) who performs the funeral feast honouring the dead clansmen. If you perform the funeral feast, **katkatop** or **mama pola,** the dead clansman's properties automatically come under your responsibility.

MARRIAGE

A person marries outside his/her clan and moiety group. Marriage within one's own clan or moiety group is incest (see case 1092) which is punished severely, and frowned upon by the society. Generally, it is a very serious crime within our society.

Every girl is required to get married and produce children, thus ensuring the survival of the clan. This does not mean that the girl is viewed merely as an economic asset, but rather as the "mother of the clan", a means of survival. A barren woman does not have the same status as a mother, especially a mother with daughters.

A valid binding customary marriage comes about only after the "bride-price" **(mata na hahina** or **kunul)** has been "paid" or distributed to the bride's clan members. Traditionally, the "price" was five strings of traditional shell money. Today, due to economic changes, it is about two strings of traditional money and between K50 and K500 in modern currency. (The highest I know of is K500). The bride is also required to give to the husband's family/clan a small fee of about one string of traditional money, **mangin.** This is known as **Laka matana ngas** or "entrance fee" to the husband's clan's territory.

Mata na hahin(a) which literally means, **'eye of a woman'**, also known as **kunul** or **kunukul** meaning "payment", is our language for "bride-wealth" or "bride-price".[1] **Hahin** or **hahina** means woman/women depending on which Patpatar (Namatanai) dialect you are speaking. This institution is enforced as a sign of a valid customary marriage, comparable to ring exchange and registration as a sign of a valid western marriage. Bridewealth is distributed or given by the man's clan/family to the woman's family during a **pokomau** or wedding ceremony; at times, after the **pokomau** ceremony and feast have been held. **Mata na hahina** is a further sign that the husband is now responsible for the well-being of his wife, and that she and her children will be under his care and responsibility.

When asked, "Is is (bride-price) a sign of selling a woman?", informants replied with a definite **NO.** "Maybe that is what some people think or do today because of the need for money. However, traditionally, and many young people are realising this today, it is a sign of a valid customary marriage and a tie or binding string between the spouses and their clans", said a grandfather. "Maybe, if I force my daughter into a marriage, then I would be 'selling' her", said a mother. "However, both traditionally and presently, most marriages take place with the girl's consent, so that is not selling".

Today, it is true that **mata na hahina** has gone up due to modern developmental changes, both economic and social. I have knowledge of "payments" of K100-K500 together with one or two strings of traditional money. These are somewhat exceptional cases at present, although it might become the rule in the future. I believe most payments today include two or five strings of traditional money and between K60 to K100. Traditionally, (and still currently) the highest recognised payment was **liman the pakona** or five strings of traditional money.

After marriage the husband traditionally goes and lives with the wife on her land. However, today it is not the usual case. By custom, both the husband and the wife are required to be faithful to each other. Adultery is frowned upon and penalised by the community. At times it might lead to separation or divorce. As in most marriages, jealousy and "fighting" are common.

Upon divorce, the children go with the mother as is common in matrilineal societies. However, the father still has a moral obligation to help to bring them up. Even if a father takes the children with him, they are still members of their mother's clan. A mother has more right to properties and the children than the father does. However, this is not conclusive, especially regarding properties which are specifically viewed as belonging to the father (e.g. a canoe or an axe). Furthermore, for a divorce to become binding, the bride-wealth has to be returned to the husband, or under certain circumstances, at least part of it. This means there is a formal dissolution of marriage. (See cases 1902, 1905 and 1906 on incest, adultery, marriage and divorce.)

SOCIAL ORGANISATION

As already evidenced, our social organisation is based on the matrilineal clan which is the most important unit socially, politically and economically. Land rights and descent, etc. are traced matrilineally, which means that the woman enjoys a high social standing (but men are still dominant). A clan is made up of a group tracing their origin to a common female ancestor. Covering the clan(s) there are also two bigger units, that is the moieties, which are subordinate to the clans. Every clan must belong to either one of these two moieties. These are the **Marmar** or **Tarago** moiety represented by the fish hawk **(taragau)** and the **Pakilaba** moiety represented by the sea eagle **(manigulai).** For instance, I belong to the **Puhutun** clan which is of the **Marmar** moiety whereas my father belong to the **Kabala** clan which is of the **Pakilaba** moiety.

Thus, we can see that marriage, descent, and succession are well-defined. Marriage must be arranged strictly outside the clan as well as the moiety group. The spirit and principles of communalism, sharing and reciprocity are active and evidenced both in the clan and the moiety. Often both moieties (that is every clan) stand together in big celebrations and feasting involving social, political and economic activities. For instance, when a member of a particular clan has died, a whole moiety may combine. The members of the particular clan of the deceased may pay for and arrange to stage the funeral feast but the members of their moiety (i.e. other clans in their moiety group) may also be involved in preparations and giving food. When one is born into a clan and moiety group, he/she dies a member of that clan and that moiety group.

It is to be noted that I have only summarised what I consider to be the three main features of my society: land, marriage, and our social organisation. On other specific cases such as incest, dispute settlement, adultery, divorce, etc., please refer to the reports and cases sent in from the field.

FOOTNOTE

1. The Patpatar language has about three main dialects. Thus, **mata na hahin, mata na hahine,** and **mata na hahina** appear, and also **kunul** or **kunukul** meaning "payment". I am using **mata na hahina** which is my dialect, Hinsal, found on the west coast. To my knowledge **mata na hahina** is the right term while **kunul** and **kunukul** are just slang

words (or colloquial language). Furthermore, I do not like the word "price" in bride-price as we do not see these "exchanges" or "payments" as "prices" for some commodity. I would prefer the word **'bride-wealth'.**

BAKOVI

WEST NEW BRITAIN PROVINCE

Cosmos Token Kaue

INTRODUCTION

The region in which I did the research is a very large area, with plenty of hills, mountains, rivers, villages and people. It is a heavily populated region, but customary law throughout the area is fundamentally the same. The particular area in which I did my research is on the northwest coast of the island of New Britain. There are just fewer than twenty villages. The Bakovi people, unlike some groups in Papua New Guinea, are still following most of their customs, and customary laws sometimes override church and introduced laws. The Bakovi people live around the Talasea Sub-Province of the West New Britain Province. The two major mission stations are Bitokara and Valupai (Roman Catholic Missions). In this area we have about seven to eight Community Schools. Despite all these whiteman's infiltrations and developments, customs and customary laws and rituals stand, survive and prosper. In fact, some of the customary laws are adapting well with economic, social, political and religious developments.

To further underscore the importance and significance of customary law to the Bakovi people, I will discuss recent developments on bride price. It is customary for these people to pay and receive brideprice. Today a man must still pay his brideprice using the national currency and his own traditional currency (shell money). Due to economic developments, the value of their traditional shell money has been increased, what is known to our national currency as revaluation. If a man refuses to pay brideprice or follow customary laws on marriage, his in-laws can get his wife back. Still, nowadays, in default of the payment of one's brideprice, the wife is most likely to act as instructed by her relatives. I have only discussed brideprice to show that the Bakovi people are not prepared just yet to cut themselves off from their customary laws, but are very prepared to protect and abide by them.

BAKOVI PEOPLE

The Bakovi people are the inhabitants of the so-called Bakovi area; they are the people who speak and understand the "Bola Language". The word "Bakovi" in the Bola language means "man". The distinction between man and woman is one of the most important aspects of the upbringing of the male. The word "Bakovi" shapes and moulds a male, his future and life. In everything he does or engages in, he must and is always aware of the fact that he is a Bakovi (man or male) and nothing less than a man or male. The way a male talks, eats, drinks, sleeps, walks, sits, etc. must be seen fit to be that of a Bakovi.

The Bakovi people are amongst the most violent and at the same time the most peaceful people of Papua New Guinea. They are very intelligent but also volatile, and can be very stupid or violent at times. They are capable of establishing friendship or good relationships within seconds, but also capable of destroying such good relationships within seconds too. There is one particular thing I must mention, and that is their ability to think and make decisions for themselves. They are the sort of people who cannot be fooled or pushed around. They are people who ask a lot of questions and raise a lot of criticisms concerning their environment and its events. When one is dealing with the Bakovi people one must always bear in mind that he is dealing with Bakovis, and caution and great care would be seen as a healthy sign.

GENERAL PRINCIPLES OF BAKOVI CUSTOMARY LAW

Corporate Responsibility:

Individuals identify themselves as belonging to family units. Family units are identified as integral components of clans or tribes, and these clans or tribes identify themselves as bits and pieces of a larger society called the village. The Bakovi people live in villages where they share benefits, duties, obligations, troubles and pain. An important principle of customary law is that an offence committed upon a kinsman or relative is an offence committed upon the clan or tribe, and even the village. This means that if someone knocked someone else on his head, and the perpetrator was put in jail without paying compensation to the injured party and his clan, there has been no settlement yet. What happens is that while the perpetrator is serving his jail term, the injured and his clan are most likely to take revenge on any of the perpetrator's relatives. According to the customary laws of the Bakovi people, the act of knocking was done by all the people of the perpetrator's clan and they are just as responsible as he is. On the other hand, the pain suffered as a result of the blow was inflicted upon all the members of the injured's clan, therefore they all must be consulted and must accept the form of settling the dispute. The customary method of solving such disputes is to conduct an informal court, whereby all the parties and their relatives are present and they must mediate the dispute. The point is to get all the parties and their relatives to witness and to take part in the dispute settlement process. Most of the cases I recorded involve situations whereby the parties to a dispute either resume trouble again afterwards or while the offenders are still in jail. Probably the best and most accepted way of settling disputes is through the payment of compensation in front of informal courts.

Compensation:

It is one of the general principles of Bakovi customary law that the party which suffers damages or injuries must be compensated, otherwise there will be paybacks and retaliations. If there is no compensation, then one must expect revenge and paybacks, which are justified. Sometimes the victim's clan would request a certain amount of compensation and state the desired form of compensation, but in most cases the offending clan uses its discretion. One must not forget that the ability to pay very high compensation claims is a means of showing one's economic and political strength.

One common misunderstanding on the principle of paying compensation is the issue of quantity. Not all the relatives of the victim of the offence are to receive compensation but they must be given the opportunity to accept or reject the compensation. This is effectively done through and by the unofficial or informal courts, not the official or formal courts which adjudicate in disputes.

Exchange of Goods and Shell Money:

One very important principle of Bakovi customary law which I found as a consequence of my research is the exchanging of goods, foodstuffs and shell money to seal the settlements of disputes. Parties to a dispute may agree on a compensation payment but are also likely to seal their dispute settlement with a feast and the exchanging of food and valuables. The Bakovi people value their shell money more than their kina and toea.

Mediation:

It is customary that parties mediate in disputes. Sometimes an impartial tribunal of elders may be set up to mediate, and impartiality is a must. If one of the parties believe strongly that one of the mediators is not being impartial, the complainants are most likely to declare a tribal war upon the partial mediator's clan. Therefore it is a principle of the Bakovi customary law that disputing parties should mediate to come up with an acceptable solution which must be bilaterally accepted and the mediators must always be impartial.

LAND

The most valuable asset of Bakovi life, land, according to Bakovi customary law, is owned by clans, and individuals cannot own land as such. They can use and cultivate land, but they cannot own it outright. All the land of each clan is held in trust by the eldest surviving members of these clans. Land according to Bakovi customary laws may be sold, given as gifts, or temporarily acquired or given away by the eldest surviving man or male, but only after the advice and consent of all the eldest and most prominent male members of the clan have been given.

It is a well-established Bakovi customary law rule that the trees and personal property planted or made available on clan land remain at all times the property of the planter or maker. This means that kinsmen have no right to claim that trees are common property merely because they were planted on land which belongs to their clan. They may take nuts or use the fruits of these trees, but the owner must always be informed. It is irrelevant when the owner is told so long as he does not find out himself. If a man builds a house on clan land, the house is the property of the builder according to customary law.

Another point worth mentioning is the right to have access to roads and passages which definitely go through other people's land to your own land. This is a right which is well-recognised in Bakovi customary law. This means that people can travel through other people's land to get their supply of fresh water from sources definitely not within their own land. Only traditional enemies do not have the freedom and right to have access to roads and passages which go through their enemies' land.

SUCCESSION TO PROPERTY

Usually the eldest sons inherit their father's personal property on behalf of their younger brothers. The sisters inherit nothing. If the deceased was in possession or holding clan property, it would pass to the eldest surviving member of the clan. Usually the eldest son is to hold all property, but the trend is to have all property in the hands of someone who is the oldest clan member until such time that the eldest son is old enough to carry the burden. Of course, according to Bakovi customary laws, the eldest son succeeds to or acquires all his father's duties, obligations, or liabilities. and benefits and rights.

Reefs, Seas, Harbours and Beaches:

It is a well-established rule of Bakovi customary law that reefs, seas, harbours, beaches and stones in the sea or on the beaches are owned property of certain clans. If someone fishes on someone's sea grounds, reefs, etc., he or she is bound to be shouted at or chased away and later ordered to pay compensation. This particular customary rule becomes very important when one of the owners of a reef, harbour, beach or any other sea property dies. Here no fishing whatsoever will be tolerated until the taboo is lifted by a big feast.

STATUS OF OFFENDER AND VICTIM

Status under Bakovi customary law is very relevant and is an important mitigating factor which must be taken into account when settling disputes. It operates like this: if the offender is a village big man or a very close relative of a big man, then one would expect the penalties not to be really hard. This is because if the offender is of a very high status, then he is bound to suffer shame, economic, social and political sanctions. On the other hand, if the victim is of a very low status, then you expect the penalties to be very tough.

PAYBACKS

It is a recognised and accepted rule of Bakovi customary law that for every damage or injury suffered, similar or worse damages or injuries must be inflicted on those who inflicted the original damages. For every act there must be paybacks, retaliation or revenge, and all the time more and more damages and injuries are suffered by both parties. The importance or significance of the principle of payback is that if a dispute is not settled as soon as possible, then one must expect more trouble.

BRIDE PRICE

This is one of the most interesting aspects of Bakovi customary law. Bride price payment is a must because it is a form of debt and a show of wealth and power. Today this has not changed much. If bride price is not yet paid, then it is a valid ground for divorce. In such situations, the wife's family can come anytime and take her back, and she is bound to follow her family's instructions. Today, bride price payments are being commercialised, but the traditional currency of shell money still plays a major role in it. In most cases, people choose freely to pay very high bride prices to show their wealth.

CHILD CUSTODY

The customary law principle here is for the father's side to adopt or take custody of the children of a dissolved marriage or separation move. If the mother's family raise the children of a dissolved or unstable marriage, then they shall be compensated for it, but the rule is that the father has the sole right to take custody of his children. This rule is a reflection of the Bakovi patrilineal kinship system, mainly that the children of a marriage automatically acquire property and rights over land on their father's side. The mother's side always agrees to collect compensation from the father's side because they know by customary law, custody goes to the father and, too, they know that they cannot offer much to them in terms of land and other property rights.

ADULTERY

This is an offence committed directly against the husband himself, the whole of his clan, and the wife's clan. It is seen as an offence committed on personal property belonging to the wife's husband and his clan. To the wife's clan it is a disgrace and a shame. There would be trouble and bloodshed if compensation is not paid promptly. The husband's clan have certain rights over the wife simply because they have paid the bride price and, in addition, the offence of adultery was committed on their kinsman's personal property. Compensation here is a must.

SUMMARY OF PRINCIPLES OF CUSTOMARY LAW

1. Payback is a principle of Bakovi customary law.

2. Wrongs, damages, or injuries are considered to be inflicted on a whole clan or tribe regardless of who actually suffered physical damages.

3. Land is owned by the clan or tribe.

4. Neutral forums for airing of grievances.

5. Exchange of goods and shell money as part of settlement.

6. Mediation as a form of conflict management.

7. Parties to a dispute correspond or relay messages to avoid confrontation (third party acts as a messenger).

8. No attempt to work out who is right and who is wrong but rather to settle the dispute.

9. No distinction between criminal and civil wrongs.

10. Eldest son inherits property on behalf of his brothers and sisters.

11. A promise is a promise and must be fulfilled.

12. Trees planted on customary land which is owned by the tribe as a whole are the property of the planter.

13. Every kinsman has the right to cultivate and use his clan's land.

14. No ordinary clansman can sell his clan's land. Only the eldest member of a clan may sell his clan's land after full consultation with the other elders of his clan.

VUNAMAMI (Tolai)

EAST NEW BRITAIN PROVINCE

Jennifer Totabu

INTRODUCTION

Research was conducted in Vunamami situated in the Kokopo area of the East New Britain Province about 37 kilometres from the main town of Rabaul. Vunamami itself has a population of 1,000-2,000 people, although the whole Kokopo area has more. The research was mainly concerned with the customary laws of the Tolai people. It was centred in Vunamami/Kokopo constituency. However, research was restricted to the Kokopo area only: The Rabaul and North Coast areas were not included.

Methods used for research included interviews, listening to discussions among older women concerning any disputes they were involved in, checking of old Village and District Court records, and actually attending cases. Informants were mostly old people from the village, Village and District Court officials, and some younger people who were involved in some past conflicts.

CUSTOMARY LAWS CONCERNING LAND

Land Ownership

Land is considered to be the most valuable property among the Tolai people. A whole village may be situated on a large piece of land, but the land is divided into strips of land which are then owned by different clans of the village. This customary ownership of land includes the surrounding areas of the village where gardening activities and business activities are conducted, and also the vast jungle that is left untouched. However, there are pieces of land that are not clan-owned but are owned by the society, e.g. the local government area and the mission area. There is also land that is owned by a business group. Such land is left untouched by the various clans.

On the other hand, in the early 1970's, people started taking back plantation land that was previously foreign-owned or owned by the government. This land was divided into smaller strips or blocks and given to the people; however, the people had to invest certain amounts of money into the group owning the plantation land before they could be given the land. These blocks of land are then family-owned, not clan-owned. It would be clan-owned if the clan itself invested some money for it, but here the family or individual was involved in the investment.

Thus traditional land is clan-owned, that is, the immediate territory surrounding the village as well as the untouched jungle or forests. Some land is society-owned, that is, the mission area, and some land can be individually owned through investment, that is, plantation land.

Land Tenure:

Land is considered free for use for normal gardening purposes. Anyone from any clan can garden or any part of customarily-owned lands provided he/she is given permission by the person in charge of that area of land. This is not strictly necessary, but this is a sign of respect to people with gardens nearby. On the whole, you can garden anywhere you like. Apart from gardening; fishing, hunting and collecting firewood is completely free provided you respect what is being planted nearby. This is normally allowed because it doesn't mean permanent ownership of the land being used.

However, customary law restrictions become evident if people from other clans want to plant crops like cocoa, coconuts, betelnuts and other cash crops that may be permanent. Thus, the use of land that belongs to another clan only involves short-term purposes, that is mainly fishing, gardening, and collecting materials. However, trees or timber are clan-owned, and permission has to be sought before members of other clans touch them. Any damage done to another clan's land results in compensation.

Land which is not clan-owned is available for public use. On the other hand, people who are in the clan have the right and freedom to use whatever their clan owns, provided they don't misuse or overuse it. Equal rights are acquired at this stage. However, in a clan structure, one can always identify customarily recognized families and others who make up the clan. For permanent land use, for example for planting coconuts or cocoa, to avoid conflict and confusion, it is customary for consultation to take place before anything is done. The removal of land-marks to extend land is also strictly prohibited.

Inheritance and Succession to Land:

Since land is valued, there are always problems over inheritance and succession. In all cases, offspring born within the mother's clan have the right to own and succeed to that right from either the mothers or the maternal uncles. However, there are particular or rare cases where land can be inherited and succeeded to from the father:

1. A situation where a Tolai man marries a non-Tolai woman and has children. That woman and her children have the right to garden or collect raw materials from the territory of the father's clan. However, they have no birthright ownership of that land and therefore, special conditions have to be met before succession is given to the children; if they promise to abide by the rules of the clan, such as staying and helping the clan with any business and respecting the clan elders. They will have to have the approval of the birthright clan members before they can do anything permanent on the land. In cases where a Tolai woman marries a non-Tolai man, the offspring born still have the right to own and succeed to the right from the mothers or uncles.

2. A situation arises where the mother's clan has a dispute with the mother and no one backs her up to allocate her any clan-owned land. In this case, if the father's clan is kind enough, it may allocate him a piece of land which he has to buy, normally with shell money, depending on the amount they charge. This land then is rightly owned and used by the family and is inherited and succeeded to by the offspring from their father. This land is strictly left alone by members of the father's clan or the father's nephews and nieces. Members of the mother's clan are also not allowed to touch this land. Offspring of these children have all the rights to this land in the future.

3. There is yet another case where the firstborn of a family has to be given traditional gifts during a special ceremony. This case is extremely rare. The firstborn of a family is very important and has to be given a special gift from his father. In this case, he is allowed to inherit a piece of land from his father. This land is considered as a gift from his father. The child has all the rights in whatever way he wishes to use the land.

These are some of the cases involving inheritance and succession to land. As I have stated earlier, land is considered to be so important an asset that inheritance and succession to land has its own rules and regulations. The fact of the matter remains in the obligation that the mother's clan have towards the children. It is solely up to the clan concerned whether the children are given the right to validly own the land. However, land is inherited and succeeded to by offspring who are born as members of the mother's clan, especially male members. Females are owners to some extent, but because they will marry outside the mother's clan, they have limited rights.

Disputes and Settlements over Land:

There are many reasons why a dispute may arise over land. One reason could be that a landmark could be moved from its original place by a person extending his piece of land by a few metres and thus narrowing another's land. Another reason could be that somebody uses the land frequently while the other doesn't, so a conflict arises there. There are many other reasons, but here I will concentrate on how settlements come about over land.

In all cases, if the matter concerns a land case, a meeting is called which is usually referred as a **warkurai.** This meeting is called by either of the disputing parties, especially the heads of the parties involved. All leaders of the village as well as anybody who knows the history of the dispute attends the meeting. And of course, the parties involved and any village people who wish to attend the meeting also attend. However, nowadays after the emergence of Western courts, such courts sometimes deal with land disputes.

The way the dispute is solved is through oral history. Most of the clans know their landmarks and their oral history, passed down by the word of mouth from generation to generation. Thus at the **warkurai** oral history is familiar to them as the story his mother and grandparents passed on to him/her. Then it is clear who is the rightful owner of the land.

INHERITANCE OF PROPERTY AND CEREMONIAL RITES

Property Inheritance:

It is customary that any property that belongs to the father individually will automatically be inherited by his immediate nephews and nieces or his sister. In other words, any property that belongs to the mother will automatically be inherited by her sons and daughters. This property includes coconuts, cocoa and bamboo. However, other properties such as betelnut and fruits can be inherited by his sons and daughters. Inheritance in the Tolai community is strictly by the mother's sons and daughters only, or by the father's nieces and nephews. However, in cases where the father has paid to the clan some amount of shell money, and he himself or with the help of his children plant the things which are growing there; then his sons and daughters can inherit those from him.

There is another case where, if a man or a woman dies, and during the funeral service a member of the clan contributes to distributing a few fathoms of shell money among the people, then the inheritance doesn't necessarily fall to the mother's sons and daughters or to the father's nieces and nephews. In this case, inheritance can be by the member of the dead person's clan who has distributed some amount of shell money during the funeral ceremony. However, the decision as to who should own the properties of the deceased person is left entirely to the clan leaders and clan head. If in some cases the mother has no children, then inheritance is to the sister or sister's children.

Land is one particular property that is not individually owned, however. One has a birthright inheritance to the clan-owned land, that is owning the land and using the land collectively. However, nowadays, because of plots of land or blocks that individuals own on large invested plantations, it seems there is individual ownership of land or rather family ownership. In this case, inheritance is directly by the sons and daughters from the fathers.

Ceremonial Rights Inheritance:

Each clan has its own decorations and designs which are used during special ceremonial occasions such as "singsings", paying of brideprice, and the initiation of boys into the both the **Dukduk** society and the manhood society. Every member that is born has automatic inheritance of such ceremonial rights. In Tolai society, inheritance of such ceremonial rights is the same as the inheritance of maternal properties. Ceremonial rites can be performed by the members of other clans, but that doesn't mean they inherit rights to them. Decorations especially are very important and regulations have to be met if they are used. Members of other clans may be given permission by clan leaders to perform these rites, as long as they don't apply them to members of their own clan, but rather to members of the clan to whom the rite belongs. In other words, the member of the other clan, in this way, shows the public that he can really perform that particular skill. The performance of such ceremonial rites involves payment of shell money. Every time decorations are applied, shell money has to be given to the decorator as a sign of respect for the decoration and also to symbolize the person's feelings that his ancestors are nearby during the ceremony.

By our custom, every boy in the family must be initiated. At this ceremony, it is customary that the uncles (or sometimes the grandfather) decorate the boy and give him the ceremonial rights of the mother's clan. This is conducted in a public ceremony so that everyone in the village from other clans realise that that particular decoration applies only to him and his brothers and cousins from the mother's clan. After the initiation ceremony, the boy begins to perform the rites the mother's clan have prescribed, and when he dies the ceremonial rites rightly go to his nephews or to his brothers. Therefore, inheritance in terms of physical property or ceremonial rights is through the mother's clan.

DESTRUCTION BY PIGS

Pigs are valuable to the Tolai people; however, the damage they do to gardens is considered serious. It is customary that all pigs must be fenced in and fed by the owner daily. However, sometimes people deliberately let the pigs out to roam the village and look for food themselves. Eventually the pig enters a garden and digs up food crops and destroys the garden. In such cases, there is bound to be trouble if the owner of the pig is known. If the pig is found in the garden by the owner of the garden, it is customary that the pig has to be killed at that very instance and not at a later date.

If the pig is not killed, village elders are informed by the owner of the garden and a **warkurai** takes place. During the **warkurai,** the owner of the pig is shamed and accused of being too lazy to feed his pigs and of not having tightly fenced them in. Compensation also takes place at the **warkurai** in order to make the public aware of the matter and encourage better rearing of pigs. Compensation involves the payment of shell money depending on the amount of damage done. However, the minimum payment is ten fathoms of shell money.

THEFT OF VALUABLES

The stealing of valuable things is regarded as very degrading and ill-mannered. Such action leads to death through sorcery even if compensation has been made. This conduct may also cause illness to the offender's family. However the stealing of valuables is very rare as it is too serious a thing to be committed.

Theft of Shell Money:

Shell money in the Tolai community is very valuable. On every occasion, payment for anything involves shell money. Bride price payment is also in the form of shell money, unless a non-Tolai marries a Tolai woman, then payment is in modern currency. Shell money is also very valuable in the **Dukduk** secret society. Whenever anything like theft of shell money is revealed to the society, there is bound to be big trouble. Such theft of shell money results in immediate compensation. Compensation is made in public so that the offender is accused and shamed by the public. Compensation involves paying back of the amount that was stolen. However, dreadful things can happen to the offender. Even though compensation has been made, clan members still feel that they have been shamed by their clan relative because of his acts. That inner feeling may drive a certain member of their clan to perform sorcery on the offender causing death. When this is done, clan members feel that the blanket of shame is taken away and the matter is forgotten, and the well-being of the clan is restored.

In certain cases, the **dukduk** itself approaches the offender and jumps up and down demanding compensation. In this case, the offender has to give a little bit more than what was stolen, and this compensation has to take place immediately in the presence of the **dukduk,** otherwise death will result.

Theft of Bamboo:

Bamboo is also valuable to the Tolais for making fishing traps as well as using it for floors and walls of houses. The theft of bamboo is also considered serious, especially when the stolen bamboo is used for fishing traps, because when fishing traps are woven and the owner starts to catch fish, he sells the fish and in return gets rolls of shell money and even cash for the fish. Compensation involves payment of shell money. It has been a usual practice that whenever bamboo is stòlen, compensation or payment is one fathom of shell money for each stolen bamboo. Sometimes, the owner of the bamboo demands more depending on the amount of time he spent looking after the bamboo.

OTHER CUSTOMARY LAWS

Sorcery:

People interviewed mentioned that under customary law, anyone found or discovered trying to perform or actually performing sorcery on human beings with no reason at all is severely dealth with. Sorcery is a common practice in Tolai society, yet there are customary laws which apply. There are cases where a sorcerer invents a new type of magic or sorcery and instead of trying it on animals first which is customary, he experiments on human beings. This case is serious, and when such incidents occur the matter is thrown to the public, and it is customary that the public accuse the offender publicly. However compensation is not involved here. The offender is warned that if he makes another attempt, then he is going to be challenged by another form of sorcery. This is even worse. At times the matter is dropped and forgotten.

In some cases where sorcery is deliberately performed and has caused death, the penalty is also death. After the offender has been discovered, he is challenged by the deceased's relatives, and later is also killed through sorcery. It is customary that the person who kills through sorcery has to die also. Sorcery is still prevalent in Tolai society nowadays, however, the penalties have been altered slightly, and changes have been made to improve the well-being of the society.

Child Adoption:

Child adoption is a common practice in Tolai society. It is customary that if you have no children, or can't bear children, you adopt through your sister or your husband's brother or maybe through members of your clan. When adoption takes place, it is customary that the child has to stay with the adopting parents from childhood when he is self-sufficient and capable of having a family. Normally a child is adopted when it is about one to six months. The child has to help the adopting parents both financially and physically when he grows up, and is not allowed to return to his biological parents.

However, sometimes the biological parents want the child back, so they try to persuade and influence the child to come back to them. In such cases, it is customary that if the child strongly desires to go back to his biological parents, compensation has to take place. Compensation usually involves the biological parents paying back everything the adopting parents have spent on the child. This sometimes amounts to hundreds of kina as well as hundreds of fathoms of shell money. If the biological parents are not able to pay all this, they might have to give up and let the child go back to his adoptive parents. Sometimes child adoption conflicts arise and spoil relationships between families.

Impregnation of Unmarried Women:

The impregnation of unmarried women nowadays is serious. In fact, the rate at which this problem occurs is increasing very rapidly. However, in the past, this was a rare case, as regulations and penalties concerning such a case were very strict. Most serious was a case where both the woman and man came from the same clan. This case is very serious as the man and woman could be in a sense brothers and sisters. Unmarried women or girls are strictly bound by the parents to avoid having sexual relationships before marriage in any case, but relationships within the clan are incestuous and are particularly repugnant. Customarily, when this happens, the girl is killed immediately by her father's brothers, and the boy or man is also killed immediately by his father and father's brothers. This is done because if they were left to survive they would bring continuous shame to their clan members for having done that. The baby is even killed for he too if left to survive would bring shame to the whole clan. In other words, such an act is just like the "boy eating his sister's waste" as the old Tolai saying emphasises.

However, the penalty has been altered and killing of offenders doesn't take place any longer. Instead compensation takes place in the form of shell money. Both parties bring out 200 fathoms of shell money each. Then 100 fathoms is distributed among the people and the other 300 fathoms of shell money goes to the girl and is kept for the child until he/she grows up. This involves quite a large amount of shell money.

A case where the unmarried woman/girl is impregnated by a man or boy from another clan is not as serious as the above one. The parties involved might have been planning to get married, however the girl becomes pregnant even before marriage. In this case, the boy or man is forced to marry the pregnant girl. It is customary that this is done on the condition that the man is not married. But before getting married, they have to pay compensation to the public which is 100 fathoms of shell money each, of which 20 fathoms is distributed among the village people and the rest preserved for the child. Then after this is done, the boy's parents pay the girl's bride price. In this case, bride price is paid even if the boy/man involved refuses to marry the girl he has impregnated. Actually this is classified as forced marriage.

Bride Price Payments:

Bride price payment is vital to the lives of Tolai people. No marriage takes place without the payment of bride price. It is customary that no girl stays or associates herself with a young boy before bride price is paid. This was very strict in the past although not so much today. Bride price customarily stands at 200 fathoms of shell money (maximum) and 100 fathoms (minimum). At times, this customary law is breached and the man elopes with his lover. Customarily this is not allowed and such cases are dealt with by village and clan leaders. However this does not result in the payment of compensation but a **warkurai** is called and both parties are accused for eloping. At a later date, bride price is forced so the girl can live with the man after all. Marriage problems in the community seem to be getting worse, so further pressures are being applied to persons involved in such cases. For example, a boy found eloping with his lover with the intention of not paying the bride price is taken to court and may be imprisoned.

BANONI

NORTH SOLOMONS PROVINCE

Regis Stella

INTRODUCTION

The following paper describes customs and principles related to customary law of the Banoni, a matrilineal society of the North Solomons Province.

LAND OWNERSHIP AND INHERITANCE

As the society of Banoni is matrilineal, all the ownership of land is under the name of the female plus all her relatives in the extended family or in the clan. Traditionally there is no specific boundary for each of the owners of the same plot of land, but each family is free to make food gardens or a pig farm or anything valuable to the family. However, this method is not suitable in an overpopulated area of land, and as population increases the problem of land shortage comes, thus all sorts of economic and social problems. These economic and social problems are new to the society because they are consequences of modern developments in health, education, mass media and the like. For example, nowadays people live a longer life because of western medical science.

Land is inherited by the female's family; that is, children and relatives in the whole clan. Even if the bridegroom has something, his children will inherit it because while he was still alive, he was working for his wife's clan, both in theory and practise. However, there are circumstances whereby the relatives of the husband or bridegroom may inherit some of the things the husband left in order to make restitution for shell money which the bridegroom's clan may have spent for anything for the wife's clan.

THEFT OF GARDEN PRODUCE AND OTHER PRODUCTS

Stealing is a very shameful and disgraceful act in Banonian society. It is rare, nevertheless it happens at times, mostly by people who are too lazy to produce whatever they might steal. If a thief were to be discovered, the owner would ask for some shell money to make up for what had been stolen. In other words a compensation payment would be requested. The amount of shell money is determined according to the degree of the stealing fault. Excluding thefts of garden produce, stealing is rarely committed because of the shame involved. People gossip about a thief, and such a person would have difficulty finding a marriage partner.

TRIBAL FIGHTS — (BENGAI)

Supposing two chiefs, A and B, declare war on each other, the two chiefs themselves are actually not involved, but rather it is their warriors who go out and do the actual fighting. While the fighting is in progress, the two chiefs, in their respective communities, prepare compensation for the warriors who will either be killed or injured. When the two chiefs see that many of their warriors have been killed or injured, or if one chief is losing the battle, an exchange of shell money is often arranged. This is accomplished without the knowledge of their warriors. In fact, their warriors are taken by surprise when they see their two chiefs sitting on a single table. While sitting on this same table, the opposing chiefs make a joint statement saying that the war has ended. This declaration, together with feasting described below, signals an end of hostilities.

If chief A has started the war, he is the one who makes the feast first. He kills pigs and organizes a large feast, to which chief B is invited, to celebrate the end of the battle. Chief A places the strings of shell money which he had prepared while the fighting was still in progress together with the food which he allocated to chief B and his supporters. After the feast, the two chiefs run and dance with two long spears and together they shout, "the war has ended". Then chief B gets his share of food and the strings of shell money which chief A has allocated to him. The pigs are given to the families who lost their men during the fight.

After this feast is held by chief A, chief B holds another feast. He does what the other chief has done, and follows the same procedures. He invites chief A to his feast and the chief gets the strings of shell money which chief B had prepared and the two chiefs dance and shout "the war has ended". After this everything is settled. The shell money which the chiefs give to each other during the feast is used to compensate for the dead and injured.

LEADERSHIP

Who becomes a chief:

In the Banonian society, a man becomes a chief not merely because of his wealth. The wealth of a man is a secondary element. The primary element when considering a man as a potential chief is his contribution to the community where he resides. This includes both physical labour and mental labour in making decisions, etc. He should take care of strangers, give food, help others, etc. A man with such qualities becomes a chief. Of course, such status positions are limited and not everyone can become a chief even if there are many qualified men.

A man starts as an ordinary man. He tells his wife to cook whenever people come and visit him, he helps his comrade when asked for help, whenever a young boy comes and plays around his house, he comes out and talks to him and invites him to stay for a meal. News of all his doings begins to spread. After a while, he builds a small **kabasa** or meeting house in which he puts a slit drum. This serves the people as a meeting house or 'hauswind'.

Then after the reigning chief dies he takes his chair. Of course, only men can become chiefs in the Banoni society.

How a chief rules:

A chief must see to the welfare of his people and must assist them in whatever way he can. A chief in the Banoni society usually has a "committee" which assists him in decision making. This committee is made up of the big man of each clan living in the community where that chief rules. This better enables him to see to the people's welfare.

A chief is also responsible for the total political, social, and economic stability of his community. A chief may also become involved in the affairs of other chiefs. If he feels that another chief is not ruling his subjects well, he tries to convince him to rule in the best interest of his subjects. At times he declares war.

MARRIAGE

Marriage must take place between persons from two unrelated clans. The parents and uncles of the bridegroom wisely choose the bride according to the demands of the society and vice versa. Both the bride and the bridegroom should be hardworking. Hardworking men and women thus have a greater chance of getting married. The ability of both the bridegroom and the bride is the most important consideration because they have to use their abilities to fulfill the social, economic, religious and political demands of the society. Economic and social reproductivity are the most important elements, and spouses are selected accordingly.

Principles of Customary Marriage:

1. couples must be hardworking.
2. couples must be mature, both physically and psychologically.
3. couples must not be related (matrilineally).
4. couples must have abilities relevant to societal demands.

Engagement:

After the parents and uncles of the male have decided on the female and likewise the parents and uncles of the bride have decided, the engagement is made in a secret meeting between the woman's party and the man's party. The parents and uncles of the bridegroom go to the house of the bride's parents and uncles and tell stories and chew betelnut. After a while they start talking about the engagement of their children. The bridegroom and the bride do not know what is going on until the day when the brideprice is paid.

Brideprice:

Brideprice is not paid for the sake of getting wealth, but rather as a sign of the connection between the bride's party and the bridegroom's party. It is a security and an external symbol of the marriage bond. During the "buying of the bride", the parents of the bridegroom go early in the morning to the bride's residence. They do not go by themselves but are followed by a number of the village people. When they arrive, the bride's parents and uncles cook food and prepare betelnuts. They also kill a pig which is cut in half; one-half is for the bridegroom's family and the villagers who followed them and the other half is for the relatives of the bride.

When the parents and uncles of the bridegroom arrive at the place of the bride, they chew betelnut and joke until the parents and uncles of the bride call the parents and uncles of the bridegroom. They go into the house where the bridegroom's parents get out the strings of shell money to be approved by the bride's party. Of course the bride and the bridegroom cannot refuse, as the deal had been made by the elders of the two clans.

After the payment is made they all eat. In the evening, the bride is decorated with shell money and is led back to the bridegroom's village. In the village, they do not stay together in the same house nor do they talk to each other. Back at home, the parents of the bridegroom kill two more pigs, one is for the people who followed them to the bride's village and the other is for the people who helped pay the brideprice. After the bride has stayed in the bridegroom's village for some time, the people then build a new house where the two will holds hands during the customary matrimonial ceremony.

All this process, when viewed from the cultural point of view, is an integral part of Banonian marriage. It is beyond the interpretation of Western philosophy. It is irrational to interpret brideprice from the point of view of a culture which is not Banonian or Melanesian as a whole cultural network. Brideprice is paid with the Banonian currency of shell money. It can be any amount of strings, depending on the consideration agreed upon by the parents and uncles of the bridegroom. but not more than 10 strings of 4 feet in length.

The measure of western currency does not have a place in the Banonian brideprice system although nowadays people are using both the shell money and western money. At times, relatives of the bridegroom contribute to the brideprice having in mind, of course, that later on they will be helped with the brideprice of their own sons.

Customary Matrimonial Ceremony:

Before the customary matrimony, the bride is not allowed under any circumstances to talk or have actions of partnership with the bridegroom. When she cooks food, she is not to give it to him directly. An older woman must carry the food to the bridegroom. On the day of the customary matrimony there is a ritualistic ceremony in which the bride gives food and touches the bridegroom for the first time. At that very moment the marriage is considered valid in the eyes of the society. After this ceremony the new couple can live together as a family.

The ritualistic ceremony which takes place within customary matrimony is called **wakobosagi.** This simply means "exchange of food". As stated above earlier, a house is built after the bride has stayed for some time at the bridegroom's village. The house is built in preparation for the customary matrimony which is to take place later. The house has two doors; one door where the bridegroom will come through and the other where the bride will come through. After this house is completed, the parents of both the bride and bridegroom start buying pigs. Usually they buy six pigs, three by the bride's parents and three by the bridegroom's parents.

On the day of the customary matrimonial ceremony, the pigs are killed and cooked. There will be two clay pots full of coconut milk which are boiled. In one clay pot there will be a piece of meat and in the other a sweet-smelling plant. The two clay pots are looked after by two elderly women. One woman holds coconut shells and the other holds the sweet-smelling plant **(tsiriwi).** The two coconut shells are circled around the head of the couple. When they do this, they shout. Then the coconut milk is sprayed at the couple by the woman with the **tsiriwi** plant.

After this, the couple are brought to the house by two old people. The bridegroom rides on the back of an old man and the bride on the back of an old woman. They enter the house from two different doors. The bride, before entering, steps first on a brownish-coloured pig which is tied to the steps. When the two old people come close, within touching distance, they hold hands. The bride and the bridegroom follow the old people until the tips of their fingers meet. Just as their fingers meet they shout, "on today we are going to sleep together?" Then the bride gives a basket of food to the bridegroom and some strings of shell money as the bridegroom's payment.

After the ceremony, they all eat together. The couple eat the pig meat which has been cooked in coconut milk. After everything is over, the couple are considered as married.

Customary Marital Obligations:

Generally, the husband is obliged to work only for the improvement of his wife's clan. He has to make food gardens and raise pigs for the economy of his wife's clan. He has to participate in organisations of feasts and other social and economic intercourse with other clans. He has to solidify his wife's clan in all aspects of life. The wife is expected to feed her husband and plant the crops and give special attention to their children's needs and wants. She can work only for the sake of improving her clan, but not the husband's clan. However, one aspect of the brideprice system is as social security which binds both the bride and the bridegroom in the midst of the two clans. If the bridegroom dies, the bride will still be considered as a wife of the bridegroom's clan and be accepted within this clan, and vice versa.

Divorce:

Traditionally, divorce is rare. Cultural demands are strictly obligatory, and few, bride or bridegroom, would run the risk of capital or other punishments. In some cases, divorce would cause tribal warfare between the bride's and the bridegroom's clans or tribes. This is because inter-clan or inter-tribe marriage often brings peace among the two clans or tribes since each of the partners is an integral part of the population. After the marriage has taken place, peaceful social and economic intercourse consequently follows. A divorce would upset this arrangement, thus divorce is uncommon in the culture of Banoni.

Compensation:

If the bridegroom is injured while doing something for his wife's clan, or dies a natural death, the wife's clan or family must pay some amount of shell money as compensation to the bridegroom's clan or family, and vice versa for the wife. If one of the children dies, the bridegroom's family or clan must pay compensation to the bride's family or clan.

Ethics and Morality in Banonian Marriage:

Ethics and morality are of the greatest importance in Banonian marriage. For example, a bridegroom is not allowed to say bad words in the presence of any member of the bride's family or relatives. The bridegroom is not allowed to have a face-to-face conversation with the bride's sister or mother or sleep in a house together even if they are in separate rooms. Most of the rules of conduct exist to help each member of the society to avoid immorality which brings a terrible shame in the eyes of everyone. Most of these precautions are indirect, and could only be found by a thorough scrutiny of Banonian ethics. Nevertheless some are explicit. In all the different spheres of life in Banonian society, morality is of greatest importance.

LAIAGAM AREA

ENGA PROVINCE

David Lambu

INTRODUCTION

Information for this project was gathered a few kilometres away from the town of Laiagam, with some comparative work done at Wabag at the border between Wabag and Laiagam. Since both of these groups are Enga speakers, the customs and practices are the same. The approximate population in the area researched was about 8-10,000.

FIGHTING

There are many types of fighting in Enga. The seriousness of a fight depends mostly on the relationship of the persons involved in it. If two members of the same family are involved in a fight, there is always the tendency to solve it in an amicable manner without any outside arbitrators or mediators. In contrast, solving differences between people from different groups, clans, or tribes is a difficult task for the people concerned. Even a small fight could lead to serious tribal wars if the persons who started the fight are unrelated. Such big fights are usually hard to stop. Police are always required to cool down the situation before anything else could be done to remedy such a fighting atmosphere.

In the case of a person getting killed or injured in a fight within a family, compensation payments would not be made. This is illustrated by case 2701 in which a man was killed by one of his clan brothers who did not pay any compensation. On the other hand, if the man had been killed by somebody from a different clan or tribe, then of course there would have been a serious fight that would have led to tribal warfare, and a large amount of compensation would have been paid for the death.

Compensation payments are necessary to smooth over the messes that may have been created within the social structure of the parties that have been involved in the fighting. Payment of compensation doesn't necessarily depend on who started the fight but rather it mainly depends on which party received an injury or got killed. The party receiving the injury is always entitled to receive compensation payments, regardless of whether he has any fault in contributing to the death or injury or not. This means that to receive compensation, you must have suffered from that particular instance of fighting.

Sometimes police intervene in the fights and arrest people who may be sent to jail if they are found guilty of causing injury or death. Nevertheless, the convicted persons will still have to pay compensation to the dead or injured person's relatives after having served the jail terms (see case 2704 in which a man was sent to jail for 9 months for causing grievous bodily harm, and still had to pay compensation payments to the injured party's tribe).

STEALING

The act of stealing is something which the society completely dislikes. It ruins a person's good reputation. Thieves get away with stealing in most cases, because they are always careful not to be caught stealing either by the owner of the property or by somebody else. However, some thieves are caught either by chance or by design, and are usually brought before customary tribunals or Village Courts. Normally they wouldn't have much to say to defend themselves. A person proved guilty of theft must pay for what he has stolen plus something extra to deter the person from stealing again. Sometimes, a first-time offender is warned not to steal again and is forgiven. But if he steals again, either from the same person or another, then there is no question but that he has to pay back with interest as prescribed by the Village Court or village elders. A person who regularly goes around thieving would be penalised more severely than one who steals for the first time.

SEXUAL OFFENCES

Where adultery has been committed, the parties to the adulterous relationship will have to pay damages to the spouse of one of the parties to the adultery, upon that spouse's complaint. It is usually hard to prove that adulterous relations existed so the village elders or the Village Court officials would take into account all the circumstantial evidence as the basis of coming to a conclusion that the two persons did commit adultery.

Where a person continuously commits adultery, it would lead to his/her spouse bringing divorce proceedings against him. It is always a good ground for bringing divorce actions. When there is a divorce, the guilty party does not benefit from bridewealth repayments. If the woman is the guilty party, her people must pay back every bit of bridewealth payment to the man's relatives, because the man is not at fault. The same thing would apply to the man if he is at fault. In this case only a portion of the bridewealth would be returned to him.

Generally speaking, when a man commits adultery, very little or nothing is said because through adulterous relations, a man could marry polygamously as it is accepted in our society. This is in contrast to a woman committing adultery in which case everyone would think badly about her and gossip, tending to lower her status in the society.

When persons from different tribes or clans commit adultery, there is always a likelihood of fighting, but in general, dissatisfactions are solved by compensation payments.

INCEST

Incestuous relations are rare and such cases are never talked about. The people concerned would try their best to keep it as secret as possible so that the information doesn't leak out to others. They consider incest as something shameful and morally unclean for the individuals concerned and for the society as well.

If it happened that a girl became pregnant due to an incestuous relationship, she would be forced to immediately marry somebody who is outside of her blood relatives. This means that no bridewealth would be demanded, for the girl's family would very much want to avoid prolonging the matter or discussing it further in bridewealth negotiations. A child from an incestuous relationship would have a bad future, according to moral beliefs, but would be accepted into the society.

LAND DISPUTES

Land disputes become civil matters when people dispute the ownership and usufructory rights of customary lands. Most of the old men are involved in discussions about who originally owned the land and how it has been used or passed on to the present generation. Much detailed evidence is usually required to convince the mediators that the land belonged to one party or the other party.

Some people claim usufructory rights alone while others claim pure ownership of the land. It is usually easy to determine usufructory rights by applying customary laws. For instance, somebody may own a piece of land within clan land, but others might have rights to collect firewood or hunt in that area. However it is very difficult to determine ownership of the land, since such a determination usually involves lengthy historical narratives relating to the land. It is usually hard to trace back how land was transferred from one generation to the other, or to discover whether there was any breakdown of ownership of that land due to tribal fights or natural disasters like famine. These are some of the things that need to be considered in determining land ownership.

CONTRACTUAL DEALINGS

Parties to **moka** (a traditional exchange pattern) exchange according to rules, set customarily, which have been practised for many years. The concept of exchanging pigs and other goods in **moka** is based on the common understanding of the people that "you must give and receive", but there is no time limitation generally as to when exchanges must be given or received. If one party fails to do something which he is obliged to do, then a customary tribunal or Village Court would do something that would relieve the aggrieved party, but generally speaking, they don't have many problems in this area of customary law.

There are many ways in which the exchange of goods can take place, depending on the cause for exchange. For instance, after having a tribal fight, there may be a pig exchange between the tribes involved. This is to reestablish friendship between the tribes, and is different from compensation payment. In such exchanges the whole tribe is involved in paying or receiving. However, individual pig exchanges may take place as well to build up a friendship with a person of another group. Sometimes pigs are given away in the hope of getting them back later with a bit of profit, whether in money or additional pigs, since often such exchanges are generally unequal and constantly increasing. All these practices are more or less a kind of social arrangement in the society and not strictly contractual in the western legal sense.

CONCLUSION

Generally, when disputes arise between individuals or groups, they always try to settle these amongst themselves. If they cannot settle the dispute by themselves, due to seriousness or for other reasons, they allow outside mediators to help them. The outside mediators may either be village elders or Village Court officials. The village elders' decisions are not always binding as they do not have any kind of instrument to enforce their decisions, whereas the Village Courts have more authoritative power as they are officially recognised. Thus their decisions can easily be enforced, and most aggrieved persons bring their grievances to Village Courts.

When groups of people are involved in a dispute or a fight, it is usually hard to solve, as it involves many people talking on the same matter. Such cases take quite a long time before they are settled.

Compensation payments are important sorts of remedies available to aggrieved parties, but the amount of compensation depends on the seriousness of individual cases. For instance, if a person is killed, the amount of compensation is quite high compared to compensation for a minor offence like stealing. Sexual offences are not regarded as serious enough to claim large amounts of compensations because parties to sexual intercourse usually agree to the act. Land disputes are the main ones which causes tribal fights because many groups of people are involved in the disputes. Land matters are always sensitive issues for the parties concerned, as they consider land to be the basis of life. People don't seem to have any difficulties in contractual dealings, as they are following set procedures that have been laid down a long time ago with a few modifications in the system due to the introduced system of business dealings.

KANDEP AREA

ENGA PROVINCE

James Liu Fox

INTRODUCTION

Research was conducted in the Kandep area of Enga Province. In all these villages, Enga is spoken, except in Mambal and Longap. These two villages border the Huli and Enga peoples, and therefore speak both languages. Villages are large, with about 800-900 persons in each. Most of my informants were people who heard disputes in the village; particularly Village Councillors and members of the Ward Committee. Following are some of the more important types of cases which arise in the Kandep area.

STEALING

Removing someone's property without the consent of the owner is termed "stealing" and is a common crime in the Kandep area. During my research, there were many cases of stealing, and I did not record every case, due to the fact that most of them did not differ much in either nature or decision reached by the Councillors. I therefore selected only three representative cases: 1202, 1210 and 1220.

The most common type of stealing is removing garden products from somebody else's garden. This was common before the arrival of whites, and people had mechanisms to deal with such crimes. Case 1202 illustrates the pattern that stealing from someone else's garden is normally settled through some kind of compensation or payback for what was lost. In most cases the person hearing the case (these days a Councillor) tries to settle the dispute in an amicable way. To do this he must make sure that they come to an agreement, which is the key aspect of customary law. Stealing from gardens is not regarded as very serious. However, in certain cases where a particular person finds sweet potatoes missing from his garden every night, he goes to the extreme of waiting in his garden with a bow and arrow to do justice. This is only in rare cases. As shown by case 1202, the defendant gives the complainant the exact number of sweet potatoes in order to settle the dispute. This has to be agreed to by the complainant. If he doesn't agree, the case continues on until the parties come to a proper compromise. Sometimes money or other goods are given to the owner of the garden products. In some part of Enga Province, it is said that tribal fighting erupts as a result of garden stealing, but this does not happen in the Kandep area, according to my informants.

The other kind of stealing is stealing other goods or property like clothes or knives. The same basic principles described above apply in this case. Money or any other goods are given to the owner as payment. If the good stolen is still in the possession of the offender, he can be told to return it by the Councillor. If he denies the allegation but there is enough evidence to prove the allegation, he can be forced to repay by the court of the Councillor, if they think that could help solve the dispute. Default of these orders may find the offender in Local Court, where most people don't want to go because if they are found guilty, they know that they'll be eating brown rice. So, all in all, the offender, after a few arguments, generally gives in and quite often he repays, even if he didn't steal. If such a case is heard in a public place (where in most cases it is) and the alleged offender refuses to pay, the the people present will shout from here and there. This will eventually frighten the accused and he surrenders.

Another kind of stealing was not found before the colonials arrived. Maybe people now do this to fit in with changing circumstances. This is breaking, entering and stealing, as in case 1220. There were in fact many cases of a similar nature. Although this is an introduced form of crime, it is settled in a customary way. As can be seen in case 1220, the Councillors tried to reach a decision that both disputing parties agreed to. Again, agreement is the vital ingredient in customary dispute settlement. Even if the chief stole only some tinned meat and clothes, the Councillor, in order to maintain economic stability in the area, awards a high repayment: a pig and K50. Both parties must however agree to the decision of the Councillor and the elders of the village. Mostly, people are threatened with the idea that if they don't follow the Councillor's order, they go to Local Court.

In conclusion, settlement of stealing disputes which I saw was good because when a case is brought before the court, the Councillor tries mostly to reach a compromise between the two parties. Normally the decision suits both parties, and this creates a friendly relationship between the disputing parties since no one is losing. The thief knows that he is giving back what he stole and he does not have any bad feelings towards the plaintiff.

However in cases heard in modern courts, one party is happly while the other is unhappy. This brings bad feelings. I recommend that whenever a case of stealing is brought before the Local Court to be dealt with summarily, it should be referred back to either Village Courts or in the case of places like Kandep where there is no Village Court, it should be referred back to the Councillor or a committee or whomever settles the dispute in the local community.

The actual striking of another person or touching him in a rude, angry, revengeful or insolent manner is known as assault or battery. This is another area of common conflict in the village. Case 1201, 1203, 1205, 1211 and 1219 were assault cases of various descriptions. Assault is sometimes dangerous because, as in case 1201, it can lead to tribal fighting and in fact, some tribal fighting erupts over assault alone. Settlement of assaults customarily involves compensation payments, as can be seen from the assault cases recorded. In cases where a person is badly injured, the damage claim is high, as in case 1201, where the person wounded by the arrow was compensated with a tremendous amount of pigs.

In assaults which are not very serious (cases 1205, 1211 and 1219) the common remedy is normally also compensation and agreement. The settlement procedure for such cases works very well. In other cases where relatives are involved in fighting, there is quite often no compensation. They normally shake hands as in case 1203. In some cases, people are assaulted while doing something wrong, like stealing. Such situations are often complicated and difficult to mediate, and may be referred to the Local Court. Common cases for assault in the Kandep area are gambling, where the loser assaults the winner; drinking, and assault with intention to steal. I recommend that the Local Court should not waste their time hearing assault cases, which should be settled in the villages in a more peaceful way, whereby both disputing parties are happy in the decisions reached.

ADULTERY

This is voluntary sexual intercourse between persons of the opposite sex, one of whom is married to a third party. Adultery is not very common in the Kandep area, mainly because it is regarded as a serious offence against another which may lead to a fight. A man can sometimes go to the extreme of murdering the adulterer or even beating hs wife to death. Cases 1214 and 1221 are such cases where the husband gets very mad when he discovers that his wife has been going around with another man. Merely talking to a former boy friend or a person whom the husband knows is trying to persuade his wife to commit adultery is also very serious, and a husband can beat his wife very badly (case no. 1208).

If a man is found committing adultery with a married woman, and is discovered, he must be prepared to pay a reasonable amount of compensation to the woman's husband. Since, as stated earlier, adultery is a very serious crime, the demand for compensation is also very high. Adultery cases are normally brought before the Councillors who talk over the issue and find out what made the woman act as she did. Normally the man is considered to be the cause of such disputes, and is then told by the Councillor to pay a certain number of pigs and some money, etc. The adulterer generally agrees, since he feels that he has committed a serious crime and therefore he should accept everything the Councillor or the elders tell him to do or pay. If he tries to reject or argue, then the woman's husband may get very wild. At the same time, the Councillor normally asks the woman's husband and his people regarding the number of pigs and amount of settlement reached. The husband then says he agrees or he doesn't, or names his further demands. The Councillor makes sure that they come to an agreement, if they don't, then there could be more trouble. The whole idea is to make the defendant feel that he has committed a serious offence according to custom. If he refuses he can be threatened and in order to live a normal life without fear, he must pay the amount ordered by the Councillor and the elders.

Today compensation rather than warfare seems to be the working remedy in adultery cases, but I was told by one of the Councillors that they really can't read the mind of the woman's husband even if he accepts what is offered by the adulterer. He may be thinking of revenge while he pretends to be accepting all the awards. One husband agreed on all the payments, but after two days he attempted to murder the man who committed adultery with his wife. The adulterer was wounded and received grievous bodily harm, but managed to escape being killed. To avoid such situations, the person who deals with such cases makes sure that the husband agrees to the settlement beyond reasonable doubt.

COMPENSATION FOR DAMAGE

There are many cases coming up to the Councillor and the elders on these issues. I recorded nine cases regarding compensation for damage to another man's property, etc: cases 1206, 1207, 1212, 1215, 1217, 1218, 1225, 1227 and 1229. It was discovered that people claim for compensation for many things. In case 1206, someone claimed payment from another for cutting down a tree that he claims as his. In such cases the Councillor finds out the truth, and if he finds that there are claims to be awarded to the plaintiff, he awards a certain amount taking into consideration how much the plaintiff lost. He makes sure that both parties agree to the decision.

Cases like 1207, where a pig is killed because it is in someone else's garden, raise problems sometimes, but the village people know exactly how to solve this problem. The dead pig was given to the defendant who actually killed it, and he replaced the plaintiff's pig with one of his own, smaller than the plaintiff's, because when one takes into account the damage to the garden of the defendant, it could cause injustice if the defendants were told to replace the plaintiff's with a similar pig to that of the plaintiff. This makes it very fair, and both parties in one way or another are satisfied with the decision reached, and there are good grounds for believing that there won't be any trouble.

Some men claim payment from a divorced wife's family. In case 1212, the plaintiff claimed that he should get his pigs back, the ones that he gave for her bride price payment. In such situations, both parties must again come to a compromise.

Where a case arises for claim of damage where one injures another or where one destroys the property of another, the element of intent is important. In case 1715 the plaintiff claimed damages for his house, destroyed by the defendant's action, of cutting down a tree which extended over his house. The Councillor does not directly determine the cost and damages done, but he must look at the mental state of the accused. Did the defendant intend to cut the tree onto the plaintiff's house, or was it a mere accident? Such things are discussed first before reaching a decision, and again a decision so reached must satisfy both parties.

In cases where one gets sick from eating food given to him/her by another person, he may claim damage for giving him bad food or poison. In case 1218, the plaintiff, believing that he ate some poisoned food, demanded that the defendant should pay his fare down to the hospital and back because it was his fault that he got sick.

Like in western law, Kandep custom requires that a man is responsible to pay another person for taking care of any member of his family, either the whole family or a single member. In case 1217 the plaintiff claims that he has not been paid by a boy's father for looking after the boy, sending him to school, etc. It is the duty of the father to take care of his family, and if one of his family members is staying with someone else he is still responsible for him. So the plaintiff was right to claim payment for all costs.

Another problem area involves car accidents. The main courts hearing claims for car accidents are the official courts. However, minor injuries received from car accidents are dealt with in the villages. In case 1225 the plaintiff claimed that she should be compensated for injury done to her by the defendant's car which was involved in an accident. Such cases are difficult to settle because there are no customary guidelines setting compensation amounts. The Councillors don't even have any idea how to determine the damage, and how much should be awarded. It was found that quite often there was much argument upon the decision reached by the Councillors and the elders. The first decision does not normally prevail: there must be arguments where the plaintiff claims more.

To avoid such problems, as a matter of recognising customary law, I feel that there should be some kind of set price that people can work with. Since there are no set prices, there always seem to be arguments, and quite often the plaintiff gets what he wants, although both parties are said to agree on the decision. I feel that the plaintiff acts unfairly sometimes when he claims such high payments for minor damage. Nowadays in Kandep, compensation claims are becoming common, and something should be done to stop one person taking advantage of another just because he received minor injuries, etc.

INCEST

This crime involves having carnal knowledge of a relative. In the Kandep area, incest is very rare. I recorded only two cases, and these were the only two cases I found. I was told by some old people that formerly they never heard of any incest cases at all.

Since incest is very rare, the ones recorded were treated differently as can be seen from the case reports. In case 1224, the Councillor thought that they were relatives, so he never did anything. The boy felt ashamed so he ran away to another place. In case 1228, the decision was quite different. The girl's parents had to claim payment from the boy. The father of the girl showed the great concern about the incident. I really don't know what should be done in incest cases, but the major punishment one receives is shame. This can even make a boy run away to another place just to keep away from his people. He may sometimes be an outcast. I feel that incest should be taken to Local Courts rather than solving them at home.

LAND DISPUTES

In the Kandep area, unlike other areas in the Enga Province, one does not hear much about land disputes. This is mainly because there is plenty of land for the population. However, there are sometimes disputes over karuka or pandanus nut tree areas, and mostly with relatives' areas around their gardens. The people regard their land as a very important thing. Maybe there'll be more land disputes in the future. I recorded only one case on land, case 1213. Most young people are not really aware of their land rights and how they inherit land. Thus in some cases, the person claiming the land had to give up when he heard from the elders that the land was actually the other person's. Most land disputes in the Kandep area are over bush land where people go to find wild karuka nuts and to hunt. The customary rule for settling land disputes is for the oldest people to give evidence, and when many stories told by different persons reveal the true owner, the land goes to the person to whom the eldest say.

The people now have the problem that they want some money to be given to them for land acquired by the administration and the missionaries at a very small cost or at no cost at all. The area is very rural, and if we start asking for money they will withdraw, so we are still waiting. Maybe one day we might take action against the government and the missionaries.

RAPE

Rape is not common. There were only two cases on rape, 1209 and 1222. Unlike in the Criminal Code, rape is treated as any other crime in Kandep. It is not that serious as recognised by the Criminal Code. In a rape case the decision reached customarily is always the same. The man is asked to give the girl's people some kind of payment to settle the dispute. Sometimes the parents of the girl may get very wild, but when it comes to making decisions about the case, the main principle of agreement and compensation applies. In case 1209 there was much argument, but it was finally decided that the boy's parents give a pig to the girl. That was all that was needed to solve the problem. In the second case, 1222, the boy raped the girl and also threatened to do her harm if she resisted. The threat is not taken into account, but the boy is told to pay for what he did, namely rape. So rape is the same as any ordinary offence.

OTHER FINDINGS

I also found a few other legal categories or types of cases. Case 1230 is a bit different from the rest. A person excreting into the drinking creek was told to dig a toilet pit for the public as his punishment. There was no compromise or agreement, but the offender had to do what he was told since he did something bad for the public. This is more like a decision by an official court, however it was done within the jurisdiction of customary principles.

Case 1216 is one in which a person found a lost spade. If it is identified and proved beyond reasonable doubt that the lost property is indeed the original owner's, the lost property is returned to the original owner.

Case numbers 1223, 1204 and 1226 are like contracts. Promises were made and on default, the plaintiff would claim damage. Although there is no legality in the formal sense in such contracts, they become an obligation to both parties. The person who takes goods away first promises to give the other person something else later. Whatever the time may be, one is obliged to pay as in the official laws. In the three cases recorded, there seemed to be a breach of contract, so the plaintiff had to take action. Finally, in a more customary way, he gets back what he was promised earlier or he is given other things as replacements. This is accomplished by coming to a compromise.

CONCLUSION

To conclude the report of this research work, I intend to summarize and make recommendations. In all the cases recorded, it was discovered that agreement and compromise were the most important ways of solving any dispute that arose. Unlike western law, in customary law there was absolutely no distinction between criminal and civil cases. All matters were regarded as the same, and the principle of agreement and compromise was used in every case, and this in fact worked.

When two disputing parties agreed on a certain decision made by the Councillors, quite often there was no further argument or trouble, and the disputing parties quite often shook hands, as a sign of friendship. This is totally opposite to the western method of solving disputes, where criminal cases are treated separately from civil cases, and the decision reached is always based on a "winner and loser" concept. This, the courts should realise, is what upsets the loser. However in customary law, there is no loser and there is no winner, but the key is agreement, and the agreement must satisfy both parties.

I therefore suggest that the traditional laws should be given more weight in all official courts, as recognised by Sch. 2.1 (Recognition of custom) of the Constitution. Especially in criminal cases, people should be told to pay compensation to the person to whom the wrong was done. In Western law, the state takes the action, and the person who actually suffered injury gets nothing. This may cause further trouble, because the person who suffered, seeing that he gets nothing for his damage, may try and get revenge and inflict the same amount of damage on the other person. So I fully support the idea of compensation in criminal cases, because this will tend to solve some law and order problems in Papua New Guinea.

MT HAGEN

WESTERN HIGHLANDS PROVINCE

Veronica Dalaka Amnol

INTRODUCTION

There is always some form of conflict between individuals or groups, in every society, which has to be settled by one or other means. Generally speaking, in Mt Hagen society, the main principle of customary law involved in settling disputes is by negotiation between the parties involved, followed by mediation and compromise. Finally compensation has to be made to the injured party to settle the dispute, depending on the nature of the injury. However, some cases result in fights or warfare.

The second principle of customary law is that dispute settlement practices depend very much on the nature of the relationship between the parties. The results of similar disputes may vary by the nature of the closeness of the parties involved (whether it is between two members of the same family or between enemies). Disputes between two members of enemy clans may lead to warfare involving clan members, depending on the nature of the dispute and the obligations of individual clansmen to take part in supporting the offending party. However, the same dispute involving two members from the same family may be settled in a more peaceable way. Here the main aim is to restore the relationship between the parties involved.

Location:

My research location was Mount Hagen in the Western Highlands Province. The specific research field site is approximately four kilometres south-east of Mount Hagen township, the total area of my fieldsite is approximately 26.4 sq kilometres. My research centre was Kum Village Court, which is about 10-15 minutes drive from the town. Kum Village

Court covers the areas of three clans: the Mogi Komungas, Mogi Agdlkas and the Mogi Kupi, situated in the Hagen Council Area.

Population:

The figures below are taken from the latest figure from the provincial government population estimates. The overall population of the Western Highlands is approximately 269,969. Of this figure, the town population is about 22,750. Bringing it down to my area of research, the population is approximately 1,156. This figure is an estimate from the total figure of the Mount Hagen Council population. It must have increased by now.

Methods:

The methods use for collecting data included:

1. Witnessing actual court case hearings in the Village Court.

2. Interviewing people, especially older people, Village Court Magistrates, Village Elders, and village police officers for past (memory) cases and how they were solved.

3. Looking at Village Court records for the past cases which had been reported.

4. Observing the people's life.

5. Hearing comments made by the village people on certain customary laws involved in a case when the case was going on.

INTERPERSONAL CONFLICTS

Disputes Over Women:

Women and pigs are the two important things in Hagen society which caused conflicts in the past and still do today. In respect to women, sexual offences grossly contravene Hagen moral principles insofar as the individual rights of the women are concerned, especially for a young girl for her virginity and a married woman for depriving her rights to consummate with her husband. Nevertheless, her husband's exclusive sexual rights over her have also been violated. Therefore, in most cases concerning adultery, conflict arises involving members from both sides depending on the nature of the act, whether raping, attempting to commit adultery or actual adultery, and depending on the nature of the relationship between parties and their respective ages.

Consider a case where a man commits adultery with a married woman. If they are related to each other, then the matter will be discussed in a different fashion than if they were unrelated, because of the nature of their relationship. Their clan members would not believe what they did, and as a result they would be very angry with both parties. Discussions in most circumstances would be in favour of the husband. If the discussion gets out of hand, then generally the parties in such disputes end up in a fight involving obligated members from both sides.

In general, however, the immediate members of the offender's families would feel that it is immoral and undiscussable in the eyes of the public and that both of them should be punished. In such cases, compensation had to be made to the injured husband by both parties:

1. For violating his rights over his wife.

2. For shaming him in the eyes of the public.

3. In order to maintain his status as a husband in the eyes of his clan members.

However, in a case involving a young girl, the matter may be approached in a more direct way. Violent steps may be taken because the public believes that the girl's dignity and reputation is being violated, since no men will want to marry her because she has a reputation for going around with men. Even if a man marries her in the end the bride price payment may not be the same as it should be for a young girl. Therefore, in most cases, more compensation is made in cases involving young girls than a married woman. This principle is illustrated by case 0213 in which compensation of K500 plus 5 pigs is made in a case involving a young girl.

Nevertheless, in most cases concerning women, the public and the elders don't take into account who is at fault, but only the consequences of the action. Therefore, in most circumstances, the man is the victim in the end who has to pay compensation as ordered by the clan elders.

Domestic Arguments:

Domestic arguments are part of most Hagen families' lives. Generally speaking, family disputes occur over:

1. Gardens, which may be dug by another member of the family, which may be ruined by pigs, or which may not be equally shared amongst the females members of the family.

2. Domestic animals, such as pigs, dogs, chickens, etc.

3. Foods like sweet potatoes, bananas, sugarcane, etc.

4. Co-wives quarrelling with each other for equal shares of the above-mentioned items, and most of all, for their husband's attention for themselves and their children.

Most domestic disputes are settled by the immediate family. However, if compromise is not reached, then the dispute is taken before the village elders.

Custody of Children:

Disputes over custody of children are very important in Hagen society because they involve not only the members of the immediate family but also the whole clan, because the child is an automatic member of the clan. Since Mount Hagen is a patrilineal society, the child is said to be owned by the father, and a member of the clan to which his father belongs. In case of any disputes over children, the father is the rightful owner of the children because the child is the successor to his father's land and possessions. However, in rare cases in the past (during the time of warfare) if the father were killed in battle, the mother would take the children back to her own place for safety. After the fight, if the relatives of the father (especially his brothers) do not take any interest in the children or attempt to get them back, then the uncles (mother's brothers) are obliged to take care of the children and give them part of their land to work. However, if the children (especially a boy) matures and wants to return to his father's land, he can do so. Although the father has died, the land still belongs to the son.

In other cases where the father dies, the child is adopted in his father's clan by the members of that clan. In rare cases, a child may be adopted into a different clan.

PRINCIPLES OF CUSTOMARY LAW

Moka Exchanges:

Moka is a ceremonial exchange wherein people from a certain clan come together and give pigs to their **moka** partners from another clan, or to distant relations, in return for funeral payments and payments for compensation. **Moka** can be conducted between individuals or by members of a particular clan who combine together as a group to exchange with the members of another clan group. Often group exchanges combine **moka** with warfare compensation payments, either for an enemy who has been killed in a fight or to restore relationships with one another. In the past, shells were used with pigs to make the transactions, however today pigs and money are used for exchange. Why I briefly mention the **moka** system is because one of the basic element of **moka** exchange is making large scale compensation payments rather than normal compensation to settle differences; especially between enemies.

Land Ownership:

Principles of customary law concerning land ownership revolve around boundaries. That is, the land within such boundaries is said to be owned by a particular tribe. Similarly, such tribal land is then divided into different parcels, and the land within a particular parcel is owned by a clan. Finally, the clan land is then divided and owned by individual members of that clan. However, there are certain lands in the clan area declared to be publicly owned by the clan, such as the land where ceremonial grounds, cemeteries, battle grounds, etc., are situated. Thus, land in Mount Hagen society is individually owned by the members of the clan, although there is some communal ownership.

There were two main methods by which people acquired land. The most important form of land ownership is inheritance from father to son. The main principle of ownership here is that whoever in the past worked a particular plot of land by building gardens, houses etc., has rightful ownership of that particular land.

The second method of land acquisition was through conquest. In the past, larger and stronger clans were the ones who owned the most land. This was possible because when a weaker tribe nearby had land, a stronger tribe declared war on the weaker tribe and chased them away, thus acquiring their land. This land was then divided amongst the members of the winning tribe who needed land, including the headman, who had to have a bit of everything.

Today the weaker clans which were chased away from their land and who have been living on some other tribal land with the permission of the owners of the land, or who have purchased land from other tribes in exchange for pigs and shells have now realised the value of land. Thus they are trying to permanently claim the land which they have been occupying.

Land was never a problem in the past, because people were never permanently settled on the land because of tribal fights. There were also fewer people allowing more land for gardening, etc. However after the colonial practice of buying land to start plantations, stations, roads, etc., people realised that land should be preserved and protected by individuals, so individual members of certain clans started to claim the land on which they once built houses, because they realised the economic benefits for themselves and their children.

Another factor contributing to the present land problem is the increase in population, which contributes to land shortage. Today if two men are trying to claim land which both believe once was used or worked by their fathers, in most cases neither is ready to give up, because land is considered part of their lives. Land problems can never be satisfied by compensation unless the value of compensation equals the value of land. Most of such disputes lead to a fight, and as a result, that particular land is divided equally between the conflicting parties by way of mediation involving the village elders and the rest of the community.

Inheritance:

The basic principle of inheritance is from father to son. Whatever the father has belongs to the sons, including land, however certain property may be inherited by the father's relatives. If the father has more than one son, when he is alive he divides the land amongst his sons. Most men allocate a number of plots to each male offspring during their childhood. At first, the father shares only a few plots of land with his son, reserving the rest for any male son to be born later and for himself. As time passes each son acquires more and more of the land which his father has reserved. Usually the eldest male acquires the greatest portion of land with the youngest male. No son is left out. If the father dies while his family is still young, then all his land rights and property pass on to his eldest son or brother to be held in trust until the children grow up to work the land. Then this man distributes the property and land according to the instructions of the deceased, or as he sees fit according to the circumstances. In a case where the father has no sons, but only female offspring, the land usually passes on to his brothers and their sons, or if there is no brother, then uncles. In most cases, the daughter can return with her husband and work the land which belonged to the father, but she can not fully own the land.

Succession:

The principle of succession holds that the land and property of a dead man automatically belongs to his immediate family and his relatives. In actual fact, the immediate family becomes the successor. Sons become successors to land, and in most circumstances the eldest and the youngest get a greater portion of the possessions or property. Ordinary property such as pigs, money, clothes, etc., is divided amongst the family and the relatives of the deceased. In some cases, while the man is still alive he distributes his land and property as he sees fit by making a verbal declaration publicly or privately in front of his family or relatives, saying that if he should die, this property goes to this person and that property to that person. Thus even before a man dies the successors to certain properties are already well-known.

As for the wife, if she is a young woman, then she is usually given some of her husband's possessions such as pigs, money, shells (in the past), etc., but not land. She is then asked by the relatives of the husband if she wants to stay. Then, she can use the land of her dead husband or of any man from the clan whom she later marries. However, an old wife normally stays with her sons until she dies.

Thefts of Garden Produce, Pigs, Etc.:

A basic principle of customary law involving thefts is that compensation has to be made according to the value of items which have been stolen. For example, if A. steals B.'s pig, B. takes the matter up to the village elders, and the conflict is discussed. A. will have to return extra for stealing B.'s pig. If B.'s pig has been killed and eaten, then A. has to find another one to substitute for it, or give cash instead of the pig. If A. cannot afford to pay the compensation, then other measures may be taken, such as prison. However, that does not settle the conflict, because B. may be still angry with A. and may take revenge in the future. Minor thefts such as garden crops, bananas, peanuts, etc., have to be compensated for according to the value of the things stolen. Here again the nature of disputes depends on the closeness of the parties involved.

Non-performance of Traditional Obligations:

Traditional obligations of individuals, clans or tribal groups are regulated by principles of mutual agreements between parties acting in good faith. In some cases, traditional obligations arise simply because the parties may be related by blood or belong to the same clan or tribal group. For example, if one person promises to do certain things or exchange certain things for payment in kind, such arrangements are customarily valid. The principles of traditional obligations and non-performance of those traditional obligations may be clearly illustrated by **moka** exchange. A **moka** exchange takes the form of a big feast where a particular clan or tribal group show their wealth and prestige in the number of pigs slaughtered, and the amount of food and money spent for the feast, usually by means of compensation for bride price or death. All the other clans or tribal groups may assist by offering their contributions in any form acceptable to the clans or tribal groups sponsoring the **moka.** Although there may not be any clear or expressed intention for the other persons to pay back the debts made in the form of such contributions, it is understood that such debt must be repaid to the other party in a similar way.

In such traditional arrangements, time is not of the essence. Such debts may be repaid at any time either directly to the person involved or to his kinsmen. Contributions may be regarded as a complete discharge of the obligations. Non-performance or non-repayment of such debt can only become enforceable to the extent that failure to fulfil or discharge the obligations may create bad relationships among the parties involved.

Concerning bride price, every blood relation of the boy who is going to get married is obliged to contribute to his bridal payment in the form of kina shell money, cassowary, bamboo oil, etc. A failure to contribute may create bad relations amongst the kinsmen. If in the future that particular relative needs any help, then the family of the boy who is married will not be obliged to help him in return.

If somebody dies, persons linked to the deceased through lineal relationships, **moka** exchange partnerships, marriage relationship, etc. have an obligation to bring money, food or pigs to the family and other lineage members who are sponsoring the funeral.

This is done first to support and aid the people during the time when they can't go out and get food for themselves, second to show sympathy to the relatives, and third to secure their position in the future if any of their own relatives dies. If B. gives A. K40 plus a small pig for a funeral, then in return A. is obliged to give B. K80 and two pigs or similar valuables to continue the good relationship. Non-performance or non-repayment of such debt can only become enforceable to the extent that failure to fulfil or discharge of the obligations may create bad relationships among the parties involved.

With the recent establishment of the Village Courts system, such traditional obligations are enforced by law. People now have realised that failure on their part to perform or fulfil traditional obligations may result in a court order for payment, failure to do which may result in jailing. I've noticed that because of the need now to go to court to enforce such traditional obligations, the traditional exchange arrangements are becoming more explicit in making agreements than before, and the parties are more aware of the enforcibility of their traditional rights under customary exchange arrangements.

PANGIA AREA (Wiru)

SOUTHERN HIGHLANDS PROVINCE

Robert Paia

INTRODUCTION

The main purpose of this survey was to elicit basic principles involved in customary law and ultimately to develop our legal system based on Papua New Guinea values, customs and beliefs. Customary laws are of great value since they have upheld traditional societies for generations. The basic aim of my survey was to collect information on customary law in villages, at homes and in or at Village, Local and National Court proceedings for the Law Reform Commission. These should be integrated into the national legal system because customary law applies to every Papua New Guinean in their daily lives. It is mostly applied by Village Courts and by the unofficial courts established by the people themselves. Though unwritten, customary law has been used and is still being used in Village Courts.

RESEARCH METHODS

Research schedules were prepared by Dr. Richard Scaglion at the end of the year 1979, and were administered during Christmas by myself. Data were gathered mainly through observation, participant-observation, and interviews. Some of my information came from village elders, young elites and Village Court magistrates, but some data were collected from general discussions with community members.

During the survey, there were certain problems which I faced during the research period.

1. Nearly half of the Pangia people were engaged in a pig feast in which nearly two thousand pigs were slaughtered and distributed.

Thus, many of the villagers and Village Court magistrates were attending the feast, so few cases were heard.

2. Christmas was a holiday period for magistrates, so when complainants brought forward their cases, the matters were withheld or deferred until February when duties were to be resumed.

3. During that period there were few cases because during the pig feast, which was considered to be important, most villagers tried their best not to create trouble. In Wiru society, feasts like this are a great event for everyone and people don't tolerate trouble.

4. I couldn't obtain written documents at the Local Court because the magistrate was on furlough and the acting magistrate only served the Kagua and Ialibu Districts.

To be honest, the above problems reduced my interest in conducting the survey. The informants were restless and a bit reluctant because their interest was elsewhere. Sometimes I had other commitments which were required by my villagers. These included liaison, decision making, attending meetings, and being an advisor.

WIRU SOCIETY AND CUSTOMARY LAW

The first outsiders who contacted the Wiru regarded them as people without law and order simply because there was no central place to deal with offenders. Furthermore, there were frequent fights with other clansmen or tribes. Such offences as killing, stealing, committing adultery, breaking and entering, and all the other major or minor offences were of some great concern to the first Europeans. Admittedly, Wiru people practised what is generally known as the "eye for eye and tooth for tooth" philosophy, which was a common practice throughout the Southern Highlands Province. While in a continual state of interlocking feuds, alliances were made, marriage arrangements made, compensations were made, and district trading routes for the exchange of salt, shell and stone axes existed. Traders were provided with protection, and the rules on sanctuary along these routes were vigorously upheld.

Matters for hearings were usually publicly aired through gossip so that elders were aware of the events. To a large degree, those matters were dealt with according to their standard of living, wealth, and power. They made decisions after long discussions and consultations. It was a general rule that they discussed first and acted later based on decisions made. Mutual support and encouragements were the most fundamental elements which each tribe possessed for bad or for good. That was their main rule.

Nearly all of Wiru customary law was derived from custom (accepted social values and usage), but others are recognised rules and orders dealing with specific situations which have been passed down through generations orally. Because there were legislative "texts" which prescribe fixed penalties and fines, I've decided to call them "flexible courts" in which penalties and actions varied according to the degree of offence. In light of my study on customary law, I've recognised three to four categories of types of laws or rules which villagers used.

These are as follows:

1. Laws used within the village, which tend to be somewhat fixed in comparison with other categories.

2. Laws used outside of village boundaries regarding enemies, where much flexibility is required.

3. Laws regarding strangers.

4. Laws used for achieved or created alliances.

Punishments levied in intra-village matters are quite tough, to train each man to recognise the importance of group cohesiveness. Any trouble within the village would only weaken it, creating uneasiness among them and providing others with the opportunity to come and take control of the land and property and to ruin houses and gardens.

Table 16.1 below indicates desirable and unacceptable behaviours regarding these four relationship classes.

Table 16.1

INTRAVILLAGE

Desirable Behaviour:	Unacceptable Behaviour:
1. Respecting and obeying the leaders.	1. Having sexual relations with another man's wife.
2. Responding when called upon in an emergency.	2. Stealing.
3. Protecting and safeguarding the relationships with dead ancestors.	3. Fighting without a good reason.

4. Respecting and rendering services to in-laws.
5. Respecting all ages.
6. Providing food for hungry or needy people.
7. Marking land boundaries with recognised plants to eliminate disputes.
8. Contributing wealth for marriages, creating alliances, etc.
9. Assisting fellow villagers.
10. Attending to those who are sick, and where necessary, hiring a specialist.

4. Poisoning somebody without others being aware.
5. Slandering or making libelous statements to create trouble.
6. Females making public speeches, smoking or cooking food during menstruation.
7. Stepping over food.
8. Children going on their own to other people's gardens.
9. Engaging in behaviour which would bring shame upon the village.

EXTRAVILLAGE REGARDING ENEMIES

Desirable Behaviour:

1. Killing.
2. Burning down houses and decimating gardens.
3. Demanding large compensations.
4. Publicly insulting.
5. Inviting them to feasts and giving them more.
6. Having sex with enemy women.
7. Acquiring lands by force.
8. Stealing from enemies.

Unacceptable Behaviour:

1. Stealing from enemies who are generally regarded as good men.
2. Perpetrating wrongs on people who are not really enemies.

REGARDING STRANGERS

Desirable Behaviour:	Unacceptable Behaviour:
1. Feeding and accommodating strangers.	1. Robbing.
2. Guiding and protecting strangers.	2. Killing.
3. rally making strangers feel at home.	3. Insulting, etc.
4. Establishing further links.	

REGARDING ALLIES

Desirable Behaviour:	Unacceptable Behaviour:
1. Giving goods and produce.	1. Stealing.
2. Giving wealth.	2. Claiming land.
3. Protecting and helping in times of emergency.	3. Insulting
4. Giving advance warning if one is aware of an ambush; poison or planned attack.	4. Fishing in their waters.
5. Compensating for services rendered.	5. Protecting allies' enemies.

Behaviours listed in Table 16.1 are sets of rules which villagers recognised, and judgement was based on the degree of offence committed. In Wiru society, a constant law-breaker was either killed or chased out of the village. Killing a constant law-breaker was not wrong at all.

These sets of rules fit into two broad categories:

1. religious codes (e.g. non-observance of taboos, women witnessing male cult activities, etc.).

2. wrongs against human beings (e.g. neglect of social obligations).

These rules seem to ensure considerable conformity in the sphere of self-regulation. Most of the offences against human beings tend to be prevented by socialization, public criticism and shame, and reciprocity or multivalent activities. These are the basis for law and order in Wiru society. Their customary law was specially designed to please dead ancestors and the general public in order to safe-guard their cultures and traditions. The above-described practices were directions for each individual and for the general community. Each individual recognises that his economic and general welfare depends on the attitude of the particular community in which he spends most of his life. The action of taking one's fellow to court for punishment may be a challenge to group solidarity. That was, and still is, a general belief among communities.

Any European, on his own, knowing nothing about people's binding rules, social control and order and their methods of handling wrongs and rights, thought that the people were living a wild life: lawless conduct, etc.; no centralised institutions; bad hygiene; continual feuds; decimating houses, gardens and fences; alliances made; broken houses scattered where it was safe; no major roads; etc. Europeans felt that they had a great task to accomplish in order to restore law and order, bring about better hygiene, better standards, infrastructure, education, etc. Because it took time to bring about change, force was used. Any domestic or civil matter was referred to kiaps and chosen officials such as unofficial policemen or Committees. Whatever actions were taken, kiaps did not consider them wrong since these chosen officials were their left and right hand men for peace and order.

MODERN COURTS

There are a number of courts which involve Pangia people today. These are:

1. Unofficial Courts.
2. Village Courts.
3. Local Courts.
4. District Court; and
5. Supreme Court.

I'll only be describing the first two, because these are of greatest concern to people and are those which they use most in their villages. Others only concern the people with major criminal offences.

General Beliefs about Laws and their Strength of Power:

Before describing the courts concerned, let me briefly describe the ideas which people have concerning these various courts at present. The unofficial court is mainly for the people in a certain village. They mainly deal with family affairs, the tensions arising within the same blood, etc. If a particular matter concerns the whole village, then the respective officials will handle the matter, each favouring his own villagers. After throwing arguments back and forth, they'll reach compromises with mutual agreements. This court exists mainly to protect influential persons from going to jail, to solve family problems, and to settle any disputes which may arise to weaken general community stabilility. But most of all, they deal with minor offences such as stealing from kin; gossiping; land disputes among brothers; quarrels and fights between wife and husband; swearing; etc.

The introduced courts are ranked according to the degree of punishment and period of sentence given. Most villagers only know about unofficial courts, Village Courts and Local Courts, but not too much about District and National Courts. It doesn't mean that they don't go for trial in National or District Court, but too many concentrate on the lower courts. To most villagers, going to higher court means closing out their relatives, families, land, property, and of course their identity as a person of that area.

Actual Practices of Unofficial and Village Courts:

There are differences between Local Courts on the one hand and unofficial and Village Courts on the other. Village Courts are meant to follow the procedures which were practised before, but it is now an institution with limitations and power. The villagers who argue and disputes, united by the same principles, are now being divided up. The unofficial courts are the primary basis for Village Courts, and fees charged are half the fee that Village Courts charge. The Village Courts are located in an area where offenders sometimes might not speak confidently. Their supporters are subdued, and if any speaking out of turn, he is likely to be charged. Group conformity and stability are not desired, since individual responsibility is stressed. At the same time, the distance between disputants is a matter to be considered. Example, if the disputants live far apart, immediate trouble is unlikely and the Village Court can handle the matter, but if the disputes arise within a village where both disputants live, village management is needed to bring about immediate settlement. For one reason or another, this method no longer exists. The peace officers, magistrates and clerks think that any matter reported to them is a matter for Village Courts.

Status of Individuals:

In the unofficial courts, the status of a person is of importance. Before taking a person to court in unofficial hearings, people consider the following things:

1. popularity.
2. wealth.
3. specialization.
4. political background.
5. relationships; and
6. deeds.

The following case illustrates the importance of an individual's status:

> On 15th November, 1979, the Councillor took his dog to the hunting area and killed some cuscus and wallabies. When he returned home, he brought in the game caught. The villagers were surprised and took the matter before the elders. The Councillor knew that such an offence would result in trouble, but he thought other villagers might not bother about it when they engaged in other activities. That doesn't mean that he had rights over the land. Others proposed that he should pay for the game, but later the case was dropped because of his position. In pre-contact times, fights and arguments involving a lot of people might have resulted.

Hunting areas were marked out by cordyline plants so that each hunter knows exactly his own land, lakes for eel trapping; hollow trees which possums use for shelter, etc. Without any respect for others, this man went ahead, but because of his position and public apology, he was granted forgiveness.

Village courts occasionally alter their rules according to (1) age, (2) sex, (3) position and (4) disabilities; but so far, the Village Court officials tend to neglect the alterations given. Law-breakers are dealt with accordingly, regardless of the above talents and divisions. Judgements show that Village Courts think they've got western-transferred powers. Proceedings are directed towards western concepts of hearings, so the hearings are either too detailed, or judgements are too harsh, which results in punishment which wasn't expected. This means that, when they question defendants they ask questions such as at what time, when, etc. which people don't know much about. During the hearing no one is allowed to talk or even clear up confusions, unlike in the unofficial courts. Village Court Magistrates even favour their own relatives, though they may find some guilty.

Let me sum up the above points by giving an example which took place during the Christmas vacation. Two girls and two boys under the age of fifteen were sleeping together for four weeks without letting anybody know. When the parents found out that the girls and boys were having affairs secretly, the matter was referred to the Village Court. Court officials questioned the youths with such questions as: By whose will did you sleep with him?; Did you have monthly periods prior to sexual activities?, Did you have such activities before?, Was it nice or painful?

Such questions are most embarrassing and humiliating in public. They haven't used such techniques in their villages, but Village Court officials having power thought such questions were appropriate as long as they were used at hearings. In this regard they go beyond their limitations, having in mind that no-one will question them back.

CONFLICT BETWEEN WESTERN AND CUSTOMARY LAW

Western law tends to safeguard rich and influential people rather than common villagers. Those who have money are better off, while poor people end up in jail. Some of the ideas put forward during a seminar in which I discussed my findings were:

1. Each Province should have their own customary law where judgement should be based on their given law. Any person coming into that Province should follow the written customary laws, because not all the customary laws will be included in newly reformed customary law. That is to overcome some of the problems such as women not being allowed to smoke in the Southern Highlands whereas in coastal areas, there are no restrictions. Reasons given by Village Court officials for this prohibition were because it would lead to sorcery, prostitution, poison, theft, and other things.

2. Some punishments were given to teach a person not to commit the same offence again. In the western legal system it was a money consciousness for government or private lawyers which led to fines. In customary law a person who had suffered or had been hurt was always compensated. For example, if a person committed adultery, the husband would claim some payments which go directly to that person concerned.

   The present legal system doesn't allow this to happen. All the fees collected go directly to the institutions concerned, and the person who brought the case loses his reward and is not satisfied with the decision made. The court only protects the deviants for their security.

CONCLUSION

The law's main concern should be the integration of custom with appropriate rules of western origin. In theory this would be desirable, but in practice the courts have applied the introduced rules automatically. Mediation should be encouraged so the matter can run its course and the decision made will be satisfactory to all parties. Present courts are not an impressive agency of justice and not popular because they are not the people's courts. To most villagers, it is a place for punishment.

The emphasis in customary law and punishment should be on the views given by the general public. Invasion of Western culture, traditions, laws, etc. are competing against our ways. I do not suggest that we should put a stop to it, but to alter it so that our unique laws, cultures and traditions should be designed in such a way to cope with new changes. Village and unofficial courts should recognise flexibilities and not just spell it out with words. This is an area in which lots of integration and conciliation is involved. Shelter of Village Courts should be dropped, and the general public should be encouraged to view their thoughts. That's the only means by which general agreements or consensus can be reached.

SIANE

SIMBU PROVINCE

Franklin Artihulawa

INTRODUCTION

The Siane people live in an area called the Siane Valley which is nearly on the border between Simbu (Chimbu) and Eastern Highlands Provinces. It is approximately seven miles away from the town of Goroka, and approximately twenty miles away from the town of Kundiawa. Geographically and culturally speaking, the people of Siane are more like Eastern Highlanders than Chimbus. Despite these linkings, the Siane people have been placed under the Simbu Province and now they are being administered by the Simbu Provincial Government with its headquarters in Kundiawa. The population of the area is approximately 10,000-15,000.

CUSTOMARY RULES OF SUCCESSION AND INHERITANCE

The customary laws regarding inheritance and succession to property among the Siane people are not so complex generally in comparison to customary laws of succession in other parts of Papua New Guinea. Strictly speaking, the complex technicalities that are prevalent under the Western rules of succession to property, in particular, those applied under the common law legal system, are non-existent under the Siane customary laws relating to property. For instance, under the British legal system, it is an obvious rule that a will speaks at death, that is, the will takes effect immediately after the death of the person who made the will (the testator). However, under the customary laws of the Siane people, that will does not apply. Simply, a will as understood in the Western sense does not exist and is never heard of among the Siane, though the educated people of the Siane area may possibly use a proper will when disposing of property in the near future.

Among the Siane people, succession to property is accomplished verbally between the owner of the property and the person who is going to succeed to that particular property and in the presence of both of them and a witness. The presence of a witness is very important in this respect because in the future, should a dispute arise as to the ownership of that particular plot of land, then the witness will be there to say who is the rightful owner.

Usually what happens is that, especially regarding real property, a father realizing that his sons were approaching the age of marriage takes his sons out onto the plot of land that he owns (that is in the Western sense) and he allocates each plot to them, beginning from the eldest to the youngest. The number of plots received depends on how many sons a father has. For a father who has two or three sons, each may get two or three plots, whereas for a father who has more than three sons, each may get only one plot. The moment the father finishes allocating each piece of land to his sons, his words take effect immediately, and accordingly, the plots of land becomes theirs automatically. Therefore the sons may commence using their land anytime they like.

As regards succession to personal property, it is usually straight forward. When a person, normally an elderly man, feels that he is nearing death, he starts giving away whatever personal property he has. Whatever property that is not given away before passing away is simply succeeded to by the relatives of the dead person.

The question arises as to what happens to the properties (both real and personal) of persons who left no heirs when they died. Under the common law legal system, the properties of such people become ownerless property, or **bona vacantia,** and simply escheat to the government. Like all Western doctrines, the doctrine of **bona vacantia** is never heard of and does not exist among the Siane people. What happens is that, when a person dies without a heir, his property **never** becomes ownerless from the moment of his death. Usually there is somebody (brother, cousin, nephew etc.) to succeed.

As is usually the case in all of the Highland societies, and unlike some coastal areas, among the Siane people, the patrilineal system of succession is followed. That is, the line of succession to property, in particular real property, stems from the father and not from the mother. Therefore the sons succeed to the property of their fathers and not their mothers.

As regards girls, they are totally non-existent as far as succession to property, that is real property, is concerned. This is because real property is considered more important and ranks higher than personal property. Further, because personal property is not placed in the same ranking as real property, girls sometimes do have a say in them. That is, before a father passes away, he may sometimes give some of his personal property to his daughters.

LAND TENURE AND OWNERSHIP

Among the Siane people, land is not communally owned as in most parts of Papua New Guinea, a concept which appears to be accepted without even questioning in detail. But rather, as will be elaborated below, the land is owned by private individuals, that is in the sense understood under the British legal system. The above may no doubt seem shocking and may even raise some eyebrows among those who normally and often mistakenly believe that all land in Papua New Guinea is communally owned, or is owned by the various clans. This notion that all land in Papua New Guinea is communally owned has been dogmatized to such an extent that any suggestions about private ownership of customary land would be taken as a mere joke. Furthermore, one must realize the patrilineal system of succession to property which is quite common in most of the Highland areas does not and may not mean that the same would be true of the areas along the coast. By the same token, just because some lands along the Gazelle Peninsula have been discovered to be owned communally, that does not and must not mean that the same would be true among the Siane people of the Simbu Province.

What I have discovered among the Siane people is that several acres of land may be referred to as land belonging to a particular clan. However, in actual fact, that particular land is owned (and that is as understood in the Western sense) by certain individuals from this clan. It is those individuals who use the land in the way they want and they need not get permission from the clan, although it is they themselves that make up the clan.

Unlike some areas in Papua New Guinea where there is a tendency to sell customary land for financial gain, such tendency is never quite apparent among the Siane people. However poor they may be financially they just don't seem to have any interest in selling their land. However, there is only one reported case where a Siane man sold a piece of his land to another Siane man, a businessman, for a sum of around K10,000.

Like under the common law legal system, among the Siane people, whatever grows above the land or is below the land belongs exclusively to the owner of the land. Therefore, whoever wants to chop down trees on the land must obtain prior permission from the owner of that particular piece of land.

HENGANOFI DISTRICT
EASTERN HIGHLANDS PROVINCE

Mao Rob Atiyafa

INTRODUCTION

This is an account of research done in selected villages in the Henganofi district of the Eastern Highlands Province. The research project was arranged in conjunction with the Law Reform Commission. Its purpose was to ascertain how people in various areas and Provinces of Papua New Guinea, in accordance with their respective beliefs, values, norms, and customs, attempt to settle conflicts. These conflicts range from a simple argument between two individuals to that involving parties of individuals (i.e. clans, tribes, communities, etc.) to the amalgamation of such groups to solve disputes over land and so forth. There were to be case studies, followed by an analysis of the nature of cases of similar types from different Provinces, taking into account the penalties imposed and so forth, to draw up a better legal system.

LOCATION OF FIELDSITE

My fieldsite was based in the area mentioned above and is basically the area I come from. People in this district live in villages composed of a single clan or a number of clans or tribes in the case of particularly large villages. Their social, political and economic institutions are similar to those found nearby within the Eastern Highlands Province. I do not wish to generalize too much by stating that most of the Highlands region share the same approach to solving conflicts. This would be too light and and incorrect. Thus I should like to look closely at the areas I researched. The distances between the villages studied ranges from 3 kilometres to a little over 25 kilometres from the research base (my own village, Finintugu). Their population ranges from 150 to more than 1,500.

TYPES OF CASES

Conflict cases vary widely in nature, thus the approach taken by the various remedy agents to solve the conflicts also differ widely. Therefore the severity of penalties imposed upon the accused reflects in itself how seriously the society regards the offences. Obviously, one would say that every offence committed regardless of its nature is an obstacle to the peace of mind and development of the village; in essence, it is not an acceptable practise or behaviour. In my analysis below I attempt to categorise the extended conflict case studies which I have collected by placing them in three categories. The first column, "strongly unacceptable", includes cases which are regarded as inhuman, totally unacceptable, and thus require the maximum sanction. When I enquired about such cases, elderly village men said such offences carry high penalties, e.g. the accused can have a spear thrust through his back, which may often result in death. The second column is composed of "not acceptable" cases which reflect that persons breaking the rules or not living up to the norms and values of the society, even if she/he is totally aware of the misdoings, are punished accordingly. The third column is composed of offences committed incidentally, or minor incidents. These are also dealt with accordingly. Table 18.1 summarizes the severity of the various cases collected.

Table 18.1

SERIOUSNESS OF CASES

Case Number	Type of Offence or Dispute	Strongly Unacceptable	Not Acceptable	Incidental
0401	Sexual Jealousy			*
0402	Domestic Animals			*
0403	Domestic Dispute		*	
0404	Sexual Rights	*		
0405	Sorcery	*		
0406	Attempted Rape	*		
0407	Land			*
0408	Bride Price			*
0409	Incest	*		
0410	Divorce	*		
0411	Insult			*
0412	Unmarried Pregnancy		*	
0413	Sorcery	*		
0414	Stealing		*	
0415	Attempted Rape		*	
0416	Child Molesting	*		
0417	Sorcery	*		
0418	Minor Dispute			*
0419	Land Dispute		*	
0420	Land Dispute		*	
0421	Domestic Animals		*	
0422	Stealing		*	
0423	Stealing		*	

It would be rather misleading to say that people break laws without knowing it. It is true in the case of pigs breaking into gardens (cases 0402 and 0421). However, in most cases the accused may know even before committing an act that it would be wrong to do so. It would be possible to produce a variety of analyses of these data, and more research and study into the field may produce one better than the present one. My analysis is not precise in that some cases could eligibly come under or be treated under all groups. For example, say cases 0402 and 0421 had turned into two big fights between the respective parties. In this situation, the penalties would be more severe than they were. As a matter of fact, the analysis, regardless of its weaknesses, gives a fair idea of the types of cases or classes of them which are not acceptable in the society. It is of paramount importance to add that even the recently introduced remedy agent, the Village Court, is failing to uphold the village way to solve conflicts as they are expected to because they impose fines which turn out to be too high for cases which could be easily be solved without money. I will take this up again in a subsequent section.

The following summary of principles of customary law touches upon only some aspects or areas of customary law.

Stealing:

Logically speaking, if one is not caught while in the process of stealing or in the process of doing anything unacceptable, there would be no negative sanctions. It only matters when one is caught. This is when the authorities are approached concerning solving the problem or differences. In solving cases the following customary principles are generally employed. The villagers consider stealing to be a bad practise. Thus, if one is caught stealing, he is required to repay with the same object of his own, that is if the accused has consumed the stolen item, sold it, etc. However, if he retains possession of the undamaged good, then he is required to return it to the rightful owner with a bonus for the same following from such an act. If he is still unable to conform to the above, he seeks assistance from relatives who may be able to help. His relatives are last resorts, so if they don't help him, then he is taken to the Police for further action. In almost all hearings I have attended over stealing, the property owners don't conform to the ideal rules above, but instead insisted that they be compensated for the stolen goods with money. Thus money is turning out to be the centre of compromises in recent Village Court hearings.

Land Disputes:

Henganofi district has never experienced any major disputes over land that have resulted in deaths or heavy casualties, but they do have minor ones of varying nature. Needless to say, they do have laws regarding ownership of land and land tenure and principles of inheritance and succession. The account related in these cases may be significant in this area.

Ownership of Land:

Land in these areas is communally owned. In essence, the whole land area that the village claims to be theirs belongs to all persons with no exceptions. Even if the village is composed of a number of clans or tribes, they all have the same rights over land communally owned. Thus, they are free to garden or hunt anywhere they like on the land, as long as they belong to any of the groups comprising the village. However, it is a common practise that each clan or tribe claims an area of land normally demarcated by geographical boundaries such as rivers and mountains. While it is free for anyone to garden where he wishes, it is true to generalise that the members of the clan or tribe would concentrate their gardens on the claimed area for the sake of security and safety to one's own relatives.

There are exceptional cases where a dominant clan or family claims ownership of a marked piece of land area and would disallow people from other families or clans to garden on it. The claim may be linked to arrangements made by their ancestors years ago, such as tribal fights over the land where many lost their lives to win it and so forth. When that happens then the land would belong to them alone, while they may still have access to communally owned land. Thus on the whole, the land belongs to all members of the village. Members refer to all those born in the village from parents who belong to the clans or tribes with established linkages with the rest of the clan members.

Principles of Inheritance and Succession and Land Tenure:

Given that the land is communally owned, and that clans and tribes tend to claim land on which their respective groupings garden, within each of the group's claimed land, the members are eligible to garden or cultivate as they wish as long as the land is primary forest. Otherwise they stick to already cultivated areas which they inherited from their parents which may have been passed on from their parents, and so on.

The automatic inheritance and succession of rights to land are generally guaranteed by the following indicators:

1. If the land was first cultivated by ancestors, and passed on to the parents, and this was witnessed by other members of the clan or family, then the inheritance is secure.

2. If features indicating previous usage still remain on the land i.e. plants such as crotons and old ditches and traces of old fences and so forth.

3. If a person is in the direct lineage of the first cultivator of the land i.e. a grandson of the pioneer, and it has been passed down the line.

There are some basics assciated with inheritance of land. The most important factor is witness. It is traditional that the father tells the son(s) which land belongs to them and how the land was obtained so that the sons know the history of their land. Then when they are challenged by other members of the group they can use oral history as proof of their claim.

Again, members are free to cultivate any virgin land, but once it comes to land once cultivated but not being used, the intending person seeks the approval of the person who has the customary or inheritance right before he proceeds to cultivate it. Conflict arises when the rightful owner is not informed Conflicts between villages occur when both villagers have not drawn up a common boundary. Movements of pigs have no restrictions and because pigs graze anywhere, regardless of boundaries of which people are aware, pigs also cause conflicts.

Outsiders may come into the group's land and garden on a temporary basis so long as they have close ties with the villagers. For example, a girl married outside the village may come back and maintain her garden which she once had when she was a girl, or the girl's children may do the same, but they would not have it for long. Once a girl resides permanently on the husband's land, she inherits and shares what the husband has as his share from his parents. Apart from these sort of relationships, no other outsider is entitled to land in another village.

Sorcery:

It is in this area that our legal system is not very effective. I wish to point out strongly here that people in Henganofi District do not have tribal clashes with bows and arrows, because such problems are handled through sorcery. More needs to be done in terms of research, because hiring of sorcerers is certainly getting to be an expensive affair or venture. Conflicts in major cases such as 0405, 0413, 0417 and others in the first column (strongly unacceptable cases) in Table 18.1 are dealt with further by employing sorcery if the resolution of the conflicts are not satisfactory. The main weakness is that it is very hard to witness sorcery attempts. Thus the best way to resolve cases regarding sorcery attempts is to shoot or kill sorcerers when they attempt to assault you. Another interesting aspect of this affair is if a sorcerer is shot to death or killed, there is no case to be dealt with because they do not take the matter to the Police or courts. Sorcery cases are very difficult for any one person to deal with.

In addition to being expensive to hire professional sorcerers to kill people, it is also a threatening event in the villages in these areas, affecting political, social and economic matters. In other words, this practise can be blamed for contributing towards the slow development in the area. I would suggest further research into sorcery allegations to prevent future problems.

Rape:

Offences that are committed which have the nature of a rape, as in cases 0406 and 0416, would mean death or rather beating up of the accused in traditional society. Nowadays in these areas, rape or other inhuman acts committed while assaulting women are regarded as most strongly unacceptable, therefore penalties imposed on the accused are often the reflection of the society's non-acceptance of such behaviour. For example in case 0416, in the opinion of this society, the accused at 15 years of age was too young to think of girls seriously. This was a failure on the part of his parents in disciplining him. He may have been troubled by his previous imprisonment, but on the whole he was inhuman in his actions, and to make things worse, he assaulted a girl of 8 years old in an attempted rape. If he had been caught during the course of act, he would be a dead person according to the girl's relatives. As it was, he was badly beaten, received a stiff fine from the Village Court which he was unable to pay, and was subsequently jailed for a month. In the other case (0406), the accused boy who attempted to rape a sleeping girl was a member of the same clan as the girl. The fact that he was younger than she was irrelevant because it was wrong for him in the first place to attempt such an act or to even think about doing it because she was a member of the same clan as he was. Thus he was beaten up and fined severely. Other cases (such as 0412) involving sexual intercourse, where the girl assented, and where the boy and the girl were in their teens and were from two different villages, and thus eligible to get married, would not lead to any conflict, but rather a compromise between the two parties over brideprice and so forth. In comparison, the previous cases had many confrontations and problems.

The following are the general laws or rules of behaviour regarding boy and girl relationships in the area:

1. For the boys to be hard working and responsible, to respect the rules of the clan, village and leaders, and to acquire goods (properties) i.e. own gardens, pigs, and a house, and await the parents to choose a wife. This attitude is changing though, as children tend to choose their own partners today.

2. For the girls to work hard at all times to attract suitors, because hard working girls are worth more than lazy girls in terms of bridewealth.

These rules themselves are very important. The penalties for breaking these sorts of behaviour often are just as harsh in terms of compensation paid and beating the accused as cases previously described.

Fighting:

In attempting to solve conflicts over fighting, whether it be between individuals or groups, the procedure normally employed by remedy agents in these areas is to seek the ultimate origin of the fighting. If there is a reason for the fight, then the casualties would be compared, given who started the fight. In other words, investigative skills are employed to get the basic facts straight. In most cases, the participants may be asked to shake hands in front of the officials. If the fight is between two different families, clans and/or tribes, feasts were traditionally arranged, but this practice does not exist any more. Fines may be imposed, not as compensation, but rather as payments to the court officials to be taken to the government, a practice which often does not satisfy the injured party. There are cases where people, after having gone through the process to restore good faith and peace, may after some time wish to take revenge because they are not satisfied with the decision. It may be of course, that they just preferred to do so.

Bride-Price and Women Eloping:

In traditional times, bride-price was of little significance to conflict-related matters because it caused few problems. This was because parents arranged the program at the right time with the fewest inconveniences. They would be sure to have enough food and goods for the bride-price before doing anything, even asking the son for his opinion. Bride-prices were then arranged between the two families and agreed upon. Sometimes very little was spent, because this was only an exchange between two villages or groups. The problem now is that young people are acting prematurely and thus involve the parents in difficult situations in which they are unable to afford payments (see case 0408). The situation is complicated by the fact that there is no limit on the amount due for bride-price. Thus the girl's relatives can charge as much as they wish, disregarding the situation of the bridegroom's party. On the whole, the general customary law associated with bride-price is that both parties make a compromise on the exchange, price and condition. Due to the current wishes of the young people, one group (the girl's) plays a more dominant role than the other.

In cases where women leave or elope with intended husbands, the situation varies depending on whether the woman is married or single. Where a married woman elopes with a married man, as in case 0410, there could be an exchange of marital partners, although this would be rare and would depend on the disposition of the parties. In most cases, the two parties would get together in the presence of the Village Court officials to collect the bride-price the husband's group has previously paid (if the new husband wishes to marry the woman, and agrees to pay back all that is demanded). Otherwise the woman is asked why she behaved as she did and is returned to the former husband (if the new husband did not wish to marry her even if he could afford the payment). Of course, often there would be clashes between parties with fines paid and so forth. It is not expected that mothers would behave that way because it brings shame to the husband and his clan. Thus, where appropriate, they would beat her up. It was mentioned to me that similar cases in the past often would result in the woman being shot and tribal fighting erupting, but this doesn't occur these days. As a matter of fact, it is a complex issue to be settled, however, the trends mentioned earlier are the general routes employed to resolve such conflicts.

CONCLUSION

I should like to conclude by saying that all that has been said derives from my own experiences as a member of the society in which the research was done. I will admit that there are weaknesses in the research, thus this report should be taken as a basis for research. I have left it open-ended for further study.

BINE, KIWAI and GOGODALA

WESTERN PROVINCE

Mapesa Dume

INTRODUCTION

My research on the project was mainly concentrated upon the Binaturi, South Kiwai Islands and Balimo areas. I could not cover the whole province due to transport difficulties. Originally I had planned to do the research within a cultural section of selected areas of the Western Province for comparison purposes.

The people of the above-mentioned areas are somewhat similar to each other in culture and custom. One uniform feature is that they are all patrilineal descent societies. Thus, ownership and succession rights are passed on from father to son. The only difference is between the languages spoken by people in these areas: Bine is spoken within Binaturi, Kiwai is spoken by Kiwai Islanders and in the immediate coastal villages, and Gogodala is spoken in the Balimo areas. A south-east border is shared between the Bine and Kiwai people whilst the Gogodalas are located in the far north sharing a north-east border with the Kiwais.

With regards to the conflict histories of the recored cases, some are memory cases dating back to the grandfather's days (about four to five decades from today), and others are of the most recent origins. The possible root causes of the recorded cases are many and varied, and differ from area to area. The most obvious of these include ownership rights over land, seas, economically useful plants, etc.; women; and deaths. The main principles of customary laws involved or discussed in case conflicts and disputes are:

1. Property ownership is through patrilineal descent, with exploitative rights granted. The ownership rights are rooted in the history of lineage, clan or family generations.

2. Adultery is strictly forbidden, the penalty being either death or disablement for life. A married woman's sexual rights belong exclusively to her husband.

3. Public abuses and insults and even gossip are not endurable in a village or community because they could cause hatred, quarrels or even fights amongst village members.

In the areas where my research was concentrated, there is the strongly-held custom that ownership follows patrilineal descent, that is from father to son. Ownership rights are rooted in the histories of family generations. In this context, when the owner of a piece of land, sea, etc. grants permission to someone to work it or for utilization, it should not be taken that the land or sea belongs to him. In actual fact, the permission given is merely a right to work the land or fish the waters, and not to become an owner of it. The sisters of the brothers of a family have no ownership right upon their marriage, but can still work the land or fish the rivers or seas upon the approval of the brothers. The original owner can at any time withdraw his permission for his land and seas being used, and whatever has been planted there (trees of economic value) become the property of the original owner. He may decide to cut them down in order to avoid any future conflicts.

Exclusive sexual rights of a married woman is to her husband, and therefore adultery is strictly forbidden. The younger girls are free to choose a husband with the final consent of their parents. The same is true for the boys. The strict norms apply to married women and men. In a case of adultery the accused is either killed or disabled for life (see case 0602).

There is a common belief that nearly all deaths are the work of sorcery. Fights are commonplace if the sorcerers responsible for a death are found out. Such deaths through sorcery are arranged as a payback for previous death.

For all such cases, the immediate remedy agents are the elderly "big men" of the village who are thought to possess power to settle disputes. These big men perform these tasks since they at least know everything within the society and village they live in. In the case of the Bine, such disputes are sorted out in the **maea** (men's sacred gathering place).

VAILALA EAST MAREKE

GULF PROVINCE

Hauka Hulape

INTRODUCTION

Vailala East, located at the mouth of the Vailala River along the western coast of the Gulf Province, is a large village composed of two separate villages, locally known as Vailala East Mareke and Vailala East Uvaripi. My research is based in Mareke village, with an estimated resident population of 200-300 people at the time of my research. People from both villages speak one common mother language known as Orokolo.

Research mostly dealt with the customary laws of the Vailala East Mareke people, with a comparison made with some selected villages in the Ihu District. This was done basically through consultation with the Police at Ihu, for references to law enforcement in villages, and the study of police cases. Methods included interviews and eye-witnessing the proceedings of cases at the Councillor's hearings, a study of the Councillor's recording books, and references to police record books at Ihu Local Court.

LOCAL DISPUTE-SETTLING AGENTS.

Village Elders:

This is a small group of elderly men in the village who are greatly respected by village people because of their personal qualities and because they are old and experienced in the practice of their custom, and have greater knowledge of all customs of the people. They are not elected or appointed by the village people to act as dispute settlers, but because old people traditionally have an obligation to ensure that the village is peaceful, whenever there is a dispute or a fight going on in the village, these old people may stop and settle the dispute instantly. They settle disputes by publicly calling out to the disputing parties while both parties are in the course of disputing to stop and settle their arguments in more peaceful ways. Sometimes they may interfere in their argument and call on both parties to listen to them only. They make their points by appealing and urging each party to forgive each other for what they have done. The matter may be settled at that instant because whatever the old men say carries a lot of weight. In case 2455, an old man in his sixties, during a dispute between a group of boys and a woman, approached the group of boys and asked them to stop behaving violently towards the woman. He told them that it was against the customary practices of the people to throw sticks at someone's house. The boys then stopped and all went home quietly.

The Oaulas:

This is a specially organised group which functions to resolve conflicts within their jurisdiction. They settle inter-clan disputes, inter-family disputes, etc. The group is basically composed of elders, heads and other leaders, or usually fathers and mothers of a family, and the grandparents of the disputing parties, depending upon the nature of the dispute and people's involvement in the dispute.

If the dispute involved members of the same clan, then the heads of the clan (the **Oaulas**) would come together and discuss the grievances. In this way, they can settle the matter peacefully. For example, suppose A. and B. are disputing over a piece of land. They both belong to the same clan, and each have some right to own and use that piece of land. In the course of their argument, B. beats up A. and A. is badly injured. This is obviously a serious matter, therefore, it has to be referred to the **Oaulas** for settlement. Both A. and B. belong to the same clan, and their parents and grandparents share a common interest in the land, therefore, the parents and grandparents of A. and B. come together also and discuss the matter, and may work out a solution concerning the disputed land. Furthermore, the parents of B. may have to compensate A. for the injuries received. In some cases, parties involved in the disputes may be members of the **Oaulas** remedy agent, though they were parties to the dispute. It is only with the absence of their parents where such situations arise.

The Village Councillors:

In principle, the Village Councillors (two in number) are recognized to be the most effective and authoritative form of dispute-settling agent in the village. This is because the Councillors are elected by the majority of the village people, and therefore represent the entire village, and because Councillors are officially recognized agents within the community, in that they are empowered by the Government, and, together with the police, enforce law and order as a single coherent system of force.

The two Councillors in the village constitute an agent to dispose of disputes in the village. According to the Council book kept by one of the Councillors (Tora Mapu), during the period from November 1980 — February 1981, nearly 90% of all disputes were settled by the Councillors while about 10% of the disputes were settled by the other dispute-settling agents.

This reflects the fact that the Councillors in the village are heavily burdened to play the role of Village Court Magistrates, law enforcement officers and peace officers. They form courts to hear and settle disputes, punish offenders and search for offenders to be brought to the court hearings subject to the provisions laid down in the Village Courts Act 1973. The method which Councillors employ to settle disputes is sometimes by way of mediation and arbitration. The councillors sometimes follow strict legal procedures for settling disputes, in that they do not allow for witnesses who may give information leading to the alleged conflicts, but rather limit the number of witnesses. Also the manner of conducting the hearings at times involves strict confinement to some given period of time, and some parties to the disputes may not be given the opportunity to speak. This of course is contrary to the principles of mediation whereby the discussion on settling the dispute is allowed to go on for as long as it may be necessary to resolve the dispute, whereby every person involved is given a fair chance of speaking, and where public opinion ought to be sought during the hearing when the matters become too complicated. Usually, some elderly people present are asked to comment upon the alledged offence on the basis of customary practices in relation to that offence. This was a common practice ever since the establishment of the Village Council System.

The Local Court:

The Local Court at Ihu is administered by the police. They keep records of all alledged offences, arrests, and complaints in the Police Occurrence Book. If the Councillors in the court hearings feel that serious cases like rape, stealing, adultery, damaging property, fighting or customary offences requiring heavy penalties are within the jurisdiction of the Local Court, they usually refer these matters to the police. The police lay a charge against an offender for breaking the customary laws of the people. Sometimes, police patrol to villages when there is trouble and arrest the offenders, but, otherwise, in most cases, the Councillors bring the offenders to the police.

CUSTOMARY LAWS RELATING TO LAND

Transfer of Land Rights:

By custom, there are two main forms of transferring rights to own and to use land from the original owner to a second person. Firstly land rights can be transferred temporarily to another person. In this situation, land is given under certain conditions and it will be taken back after a period of time. Sometimes when the conditions are violated by the second owner, the land will be taken back from him. Land is usually given to someone outside the lineage group of the owner. Perhaps in some cases, the land may be given on the condition that the second owner may build a temporary house to reside on the piece of land for a period of time, but must not use the land for any other purpose (like planting a coconut palm beside his house). After the given period of time, he must find a site where he can reside permanently. If the second owner refuses to move out, he may plant a coconut, thus violating the terms and conditions of the agreement. This is because to plant a coconut palm constitutes a customary symbol that the second owner has some right to use and own that land in the future. Therefore, to avoid this, the original owner is very strict in setting out terms and conditions of temporary land use.

The second form of transferring land rights of use and ownership is by customary inheritance, whereby the land is passed down from the first generation to the second generation. This is normally land transferred in a single lineage group, either in family units or on a clan basis, depending on the number of people sharing rights over that piece of land. The land becomes small plots if later children all divide it among themselves. Of course some people may lose rights to some other piece of land but may have full possession in other areas where they own land.

Land Disputes:

In disputes over land, one of the main issues raised would be clarifying the boundary lines and the original marks established as border marks in order that the land owners may identify the land to be their own. The land boundary marks are usually things like an old, tall coconut palm, an old big tree which may be seen high above the rest of the vegetation, or sometimes land forms are used as the basis of the boundary line, like small creeks, rivers, pools and swamps, or a footpath that may have existed ever since the land was inherited. These marks are used in clarifying border disputes, and on that basis, people are able to settle accordingly. Case 2404 illustrates the usual method of settling such disputes through the **Oaulas** remedy agent. The following is a summary of settlement procedures in this case:

An old man, an elder of the clan of one of the principal parties to the dispute, stepped forward and directed the men's attention to a group of large tall-looking coconut palms high above the rest of the vegetation whereby he clarified the actual position of the border line, and directed them in line with the coconuts into the bush far inwards. Having made the boundary line clear, he discussed the historical background of the land and its original marks, and identified the lineage group in the clan that was actually using the piece of land ever since the land was inherited. With that, he named the particular lineage group of ancestors to one of the parties (the one in his own group).

After having made such a remark, he asked the other party for futher queries. An elderly man from this group replied that the old man's statements were true and were accepted by his party, for they had similar knowledge of the historical background of that land as told by their own parents and grandparents. However, he further responded with a remark that, because they are part of the lineage group by maternal relationship, thus belonging to the same clan, they must at least be given some right to use that piece of land. It would be bad for them to take away their rights to use that land permanently.

This remark needed deep consideration, because land rights given to another on a maternal basis of relation by custom can not be easily reversed or taken away. In such a situation, both parties together have to work out some solution. A clansman from the group originally owning the land suggested that the other group's right to use that piece of land should not be taken away from them, but rather remain as it has been on the condition that their rights to use the land be within their given boundary line and not over to the other side which had precipitated the current disputes.

The suggestion was accepted by both parties with an expression of mutual friendship. It was later brought forward by the other party that the whole area of the dispute be cut down and made into a big garden, in order that there be new landmarks placed in line with the original landmarks, and fair share be made to all the clansmen. All members at the hearing agreed with the suggestion and proposed a big garden be made soon on the disputed land. The matter then was settled instantly with all shaking hands in a friendly way.

It is quite clear who was involved in settling the dispute. Throughout the process of dispute settlement, a small number of old people (two or three) from both sides were present to give their knowledge about the disputed land and to assist in settling the matter peacefully. Of course, some other men (about seven) together with some young boys were there to witness the settlement of the dispute, to learn from the old people about the land, and to hear the resolutions passed concerning the disputed land.

DISPUTES INVOLVING WOMEN AND LEGAL STATUS OF WOMEN

In hearing cases involving a woman/girl who may be one of the parties to the offence committed, there is always special respect accorded to the female party in due respect of her status within the community. It is by custom that the woman be treated more liberally, even if she had committed the offence herself, or may have been one of the principal parties to the commission of the alleged offence. Also in a situation such as rape, one of the determining factors that the court takes into account is the potential status of the victim. In a case where an older woman at about 30 has been raped, the penalty charged is less than that charged for raping a young girl below the age of 20. The penalty depends upon the status of the woman and how much she is valued in the community. This situation is illustrated in Case 2414 in which a young man planned to rape a community school teacher. Merely planning to rape a young unmarried girl the age of 18 years is a serious act, even if it is only a plan and not the actual offence. The value of the potential victim may have to be tested on such factors as whether she would get married again to another man, if she is a widow, or an older woman; whether she is capable of doing community work, can help in maintaining the family, or is a wise woman who has no previous criminal record. And, of course, the court may also have to look back on the previous history of the accused man, whether he had done the same indecent thing before, etc.

In cases in which a woman is solely held responsible for initiating the commission of an offence, she does not face the same penalty which would be faced by a male. If she got involved with a man in the course of commission of the offence, the man takes the maximum penalty, while the women takes much lighter punishment. This may seem to be unfair to the man, because he may have been a victim of the activities carried out by the woman at her personal wish. This situation occurs in cases of adultery, whereby a woman asks at her own wish to have intercourse with the man or even may to trick him into it. Having committed the act, the man when brought before the court of law is given the maximum penalty for the alleged act.

THEFT OF GOODS

Like everywhere else, it is an offence to steal the property of another. A person will be accused of committing the act of stealing if he takes away something which to his/her knowledge does not belong to him without the owner's consent or without his presence. Stealing may take many forms: someone may take away the property of another and keep it for a period of time, thus depriving the owner of its use, or may take away the property of another and replace it with a similar substance/object. The latter is quite a common practice in the village today. One of the typical cases of that nature is illustrated in Case 2415 where a bunch of betelnuts from a palm belonging to a woman was stolen during the night. The next morning, she publicly accused a number of people whom she suspected of stealing the bunch of betelnuts, but failed to identify the actual offender. A day later, she found a similar sized bunch of betelnut (not the one stolen) hanging on one of the palms. It was of course signifying the return of the stolen betelnut by the accused, because he feared that he would soon be found out if he did nothing to rectify his act.

Another form of stealing is locally known as **mari korea**, which simply implies girl-stealing. This obviously is a significant form of stealing. A male person will be accused of **mari korea** if he makes no customary formal arrangements with the girl's parents. For example, if he wishes to marry her, but takes her away out of the care of her parents secretly and leaves her in the house of his relatives, the rest of the people and her parents will accuse the man of stealing their daughter. This also applies in situations where a boy may want to have sexual relations with a girlfriend of his, and he arranges a secret affair with her, and takes her out without the consent of her parents, though the parents may previously have given them permission to go out for the night together. The secrecy element consitutes the offence of stealing.

To charge a person for the alleged act of stealing is a matter solely for the complainant to decide. If he wants to lay a charge against the accused and make an order of payment, he may do so. In matters relating to garden produce, food crops, etc., the penalty is much heavier than any other act of stealing. This is because it involves a long term payment according to custom, if the matter is a serious one. The seriousness of the matter depends entirely upon the nature of food stolen, and the quantity stolen. When a person steals garden produce like watermelon, corn, bananas, taros, etc., the accused by custom is entitled to pay back to the complainant a similar quantity of the stolen food crops. If the accused does not own a garden at the time, he will have to make a new garden and produce as much as he can to pay back what he stole from the complainant. It obviously takes a long time to pay back, but he will bring disgrace to himself and to the rest of the family and his clan if he does not work to pay back his debt. He will also be regarded as a lazy man who does nothing but sleep and steal, thus living on other people's effort. This practice of paying back garden produce in kind for an offence is fading away because in most cases, when a dispute is settled, the court lays charges against the offender on the basis of cash evaluations.

Paying cash for an offence as a fine to the court is a common practice throughout the villages in the Ihu area, including my reseach site. Nearly 95% of the cases either brought to the Local Court or the court hearings in the villages result in cash payment penalties. The police record at Ihu Local Court reveals that cases like claims of compensation for damage to properties, offences of stealing, offences against another person, offences of unlawfully being on other people's premises, for unlawfully fishing/hunting on a customarily fobidden area, offences of false accusations to another, offences relating to boy-girl sexual relationships and offences against the public are charged on the basis of cash payments to the victimized/ complainant party.

In villages like Harola, Lepokeral, Hiloi, Apuraria, Iari, Auma and Keaura, offences of stealing goods were paid back in terms of similar items to those stolen plus some interest in the form of a pig, chicken, etc. This has been a traditional practice and still is practiced in some areas where people can't afford to pay in cash. A payment of goods is accepted in such situations. In most cases, the councillors/ courts lay charges up to K200.00, this being the maximum penalty.

FAMILY ARGUMENTS/DISPUTES

During the time of the research there were a number of minor disputes within the family and between some married couples. These disputes were brought to the attention of the Village Councillors to determine and settle. This is basically because, as a matter of tradition, domestic disputes between married couples, or members of a family themselves, are matters within their own groups and have to be settled accordingly by themselves. Interference by outside people from different family groups or clan groups who come to assist in settling the matter, or to help one of the parties to the dispute in making a point, would only worsen family arguments.

Therefore, what ought to be done is to leave such persons to settle the matter themselves. Not even Councillors or village elders should question them on the matter. Of course, such disputes can be settled by the heads of the family, either parents or grandparents of the disputing parties, who may not necessarily be involved in the dispute. They may call on their sons, daughters, grandson, etc. to come together and settle the matter more peacefully before them.

Villages like Hiloi, Lepokera and Auma have similar conflict management patterns. No outside person is allowed to interfere in the course of a family dispute. In one case, a widow was knocked unconscious by one of her deceased husband's brothers, who was beating and kicking her while she was lying on the ground. This of course is a serious assault to the woman, but the general public may not interfere until the brothers or relatives of the widow come to aid her. This is because it is a customary rule that no person outside the family will direct the husband's party in their dispute, because he has no right to do so, and because, as bride price was paid, beating her like that would not really matter.

One may wonder if the brother of the deceased husband had the right to beat her like that. As long as the bride price was paid, there is no question about it. Otherwise if the bride price had not been paid, the brothers of the deceased husband would have had no right to do so. Also, it may depend entirely on why she receives such a punishment, whether she is not co-operating or is refusing to do the house work that is expected of her (as in this case). If this were the case, then the general public may express their concern that she deserves such a punishment for not washing clothes, cooking food, etc.

BREACH OF OTHER CUSTOMARY LAWS

Sexual Offenses:

It is an offense for a boy to have sexual relations with a girl, especially when they are immature. If both consent to having sexual relations, when they both are found, they may be regarded as an engaged couple by custom. This is basically because both of them have already shown interest in each other and are both apparently willing to be married. To name the couple as an engaged couple would give protection to the girl from being sexually exploited by another male.

If the girl consents to having sexual relations with another male then the girl has committed a very serious crime (together with the second male). This is because, if the girl becomes pregnant, there is going to be an argument. This first male may refuse to marry her, because he may claim that he was not the only one responsible for the girl's pregnancy, having in mind that the girl also had sexual relations with the second male. In such situations, things might become more complicated, and the case may not be easily solved when brought to the Councillor's hearing. This situation is illustrated in Cases 2421 and 2422. Now, the girl is left with the child with no father.

To avoid bringing this kind of problem about, the Councillors during the recent meeting made a rule that, "Whenever a boy and a girl are found having sexual relations, they will get married on that occasion". It has been a problem that the parents of the girl and the Councillors find very difficult to settle. After all, other things may occur after the incident and the couple's engagement. All the village people at the gathering accepted the new rule by the Councillors, and now the rule is fully enforced.

Breach of the Peace:

The offence of breach of the peace may occur in many forms. Some of the common ways in which this is observed occur when a person unlawfully enters the premises of another, or when a person in the middle of the night shouts around the village thus disturbing the whole village, or when someone tries to pick a fight with another person in a public gathering, or when someone damages public property. These are offences of breach of peace where by custom a Councillor may publicly accuse and condemn the offender. This would disgrace the offender before the eyes of the community, thus discouraging the offender from committing similar acts in the future. Accusing another of an offence may take in two forms:

1. The complainant may publicly accuse by standing out in the middle of the village and calling out the suspected person's name, or rather direct his call to the suspect and start to give an account of what he had done. The complainant in such case may want the suspect to reply in an argument so that he may publicly condemn him and degrade him, thus disgracing him. This sometimes may result in violent confrontation between the two parties.
2. In the second form of accusation, the complainant may secretly make accusations before another group of men. Then one of them may later tell the person being accused of what he had heard.

In such cases, both in the first and the second forms, the accused person may seek the Councillor's aid to call upon the complainant before the hearing for determining the validity of his/her accusations.

SORCERY

As practised in many places throughout the province and nationwide, sorcery is a serious offence. Any person who uses the power of sorcery and other evil practices to harm another will have to be processed accordingly by a court of law, and may be fined by the court, upon conviction. Subject to the Sorcery Act 1971, it is against the law to practice sorcery other than innocent sorcery. Under Part III of the Act, any person who performs such an act of forbidden sorcery is accordingly prosecuted. The courts, both the Village Councillor's constituted courts and the Local Court at Ihu apply the relevant provisions of the Sorcery Act when dealing with matters of sorcery. Normally, such disputes are brought before the Local Court hearings at Ihu, because the Councillors feel that they have no jurisdiction over such matters. Though the Local Court at Ihu is an official court, customary principles of dealing with such matters are applied in determining the case.

In villages nowadays, any person practicing or threatening other people with sorcery is seriously dealt with, because people believe this is a danger to the community. Sorcerers may be threatened to be murdered in cold blood with an axe or a knife by the people on whom they make sorcery. This has occured at least once in the village (Case 2444). In that case, the sorcerer was accused of poisoning the child of a man with whom he had previously had a land dispute:

> The alleged sorcerer was seen standing outside the back of the man's house holding a strange object which looked more like a small round stone. He threw it into the window of the house, and it landed inside the family sleeping room. This object was identified as a sorcerer's property to poison another person.
>
> All these actions were observed by an old woman who was sitting in the corner of her house on the verandah next to the child's house. The next day when the child became sick, the old woman related what she had observed the other day to the child's father. He was so angry that he ran into the room, picked up a bayonet, and ran straight to the sorcerer's house to murder him. He obviously wanted to murder him, because they have been enemies for a long time. The sorcerer noticed him coming and ran into the tall grass under the coconut palms.
>
> The matter then was referred to the police at Ihu, and the sorcerer was brought to the court by the police. At the hearing, the sorcerer admitted committing the alleged act of sorcery. The Court ordered him to pay K10.00 compensation payment to the victim's party, and warned him not to perform his evil practices again.

It was stated that this practice of threatening or attempting to murder sorcerers is acceptable to the people of the community, and is becoming common throughout the area. Therefore, anyone found performing acts of sorcery is given no chance or escape when confronted by his opponents. It is hoped that such attitudes may eliminate the practice of sorcery and bring peace and harmonious life, and establish a protective community.

PROBLEMS/DIFFICULTIES ENCOUNTERED IN THE RESEARCH WORK

In doing the research, I personally have experienced a number of problems, thus creating difficulties in meeting the requirements of the research project. One of the first main problem areas that I encountered was in the context of collection of information relating to the terms of reference as outlined on the research project forms. This problem involved, firstly, inadequate and improperly constituted dispute settling agents in the research area. This contributed to the problems of lack of sufficient information. Though the two Councillors of the village constituted an agent for settling disputes, they lacked the capacity and ability to properly record the alleged disputing matters in the past. The second problem within this area was that the Councillors were not as co-operative as I expected. This was probably because they were either reluctant to release as much information as was required or may have thought that feeding me such information would advance my education where I would receive the benefit while they would get nothing. This kind of attitude among the Councillors made things difficult for me to obtain as much information as was required. The third problem experienced within this area was that, even if I attempted to interview a number of old men from the village, and tried to collect as much information as I could, I found little co-operation. Old men were quite reluctant to release information, and some even claimed money payments before they provided information. I depended very much upon my parents, and attended every case hearing in the village and recorded the information myself.

The second problem area was that I had my own family commitments. Because I was in the village, I was expected by my parents, relatives and the village people to contribute towards working in the community, and to take part in some of the important activities organised by the people. With this, I spent some time in this work, and so I was somewhat ineffective in doing the research. Otherwise, overall, I have quite enjoyed the project work, and was glad that I learned a lot from my people and at the same time enjoyed working for the Commission.

SOME PROPOSED RECOMMENDATIONS TO RECTIFY THE PROBLEM AREAS

It is in the conclusion of this report that I feel it necessary to place my personal recommendations in line with the research carried out to rectify some of the problem areas of my research site, in order that, perhaps, whoever it may be who design policies to administer services, especially in the field of administering justice to this area, may find it worth giving some thought on the following proposals in various aspects of administering justice:

Establish a Village Court System:

There is a need for a properly constituted dispute settling agent in substituting for the present "Councillor's Constituted Agent". At present, the two Councillors take the heavy burden of enforcing law and order, arresting offenders, searching for offenders to bring along to court, and determining cases at the hearings in which they also play the role of Village Court Magistrates. This of course is a difficult task to administer justice at such a local level of society where the people are long adjusted to their own lifestyle and are not so familiar with the introduced system of dispute settlement. It is therefore, my first recommendation that, subject to the expressed needs of the Village Court Act 1973, such a body ought to be established so as to effectively and more efficiently administer the work of the judiciary in the village. This would also share the burden of the Councillor's work.

Application of Customary Principles of Dispute Settlement:

There have been numerous occasions whereby the courts apply semi-strict legal procedures in settling disputes in the village. Strict principles of settling disputes were applied in the proceedings, whereas the court ought to be confined to the application of customary principles of settling disputes, either by way of mediation or arbitration. Though some of these methods are applied in one way or the other, in practice the essential elements that make the methods work are not observed. Therefore, it is my second recommendation that the conduct of proceedings in such courts need to be encompassed by the customary scene of dispute settlement.

Imposition of Customary Valuables Rather Than Cash for Fines/Penalties:

This, of course, is one of the most serious problems faced by the people. In most cases, whether in criminal or civil matters, the payments to meet the penalties imposed are usually cash. Some offenders cannot afford to pay, and therefore ought to be given the chance to pay the penalties in terms of customary goods like pigs, chickens or shell money. It must be decided by both parties in a dispute, not necessarily by the courts.

AROMA COAST

CENTRAL PROVINCE

Wari Iamo

INTRODUCTION

This paper examines aspects of the customary law of the Aroma people. The research was conducted in Paramana Village, located at Keppel Point on the coast of Aroma between Hood Lagoon and Kupiano. The people speak Keakalo, the language spoken throughout the Aroma coast.

TRADITIONAL DISPUTE MANAGEMENT

Dispute management techniques depend upon the relationship between the parties to a dispute. For members of the same social group or related groups, a traditional moot or village meeting was commonly held to settle certain village problems. Most cases that were heard in the traditional moot involved used rights over produce and stealing plant produce such as betel nut, coconuts, bananas, watermelons, yams, tapioca, etc. Disputes between members of different social groups with no consaguineal or affinal ties sometimes escalated into a customarily-regulated fight called **veala.** **Veala** fights generally occured over women and land problems.

The Traditional Moot:

The traditional moot almost resembles the Village Court structure. A village chief acts as head or chairman of the moot, with six headmen representing different clans of the village assisting as **katimani,** who imitate policemen. Usually, the village chief is more authoritarian in handing down decisions. His decisions are enforced by the six **katimani** who act as policemen. To some extent they influence the chief in decision making.

The traditional moot comes in force or operation within a specified period of 8-12 months. During this period known as **rova,** a restriction on plant produce, i.e. betel nuts, coconuts and garden crops is administered by the chief and the village people. The rules of the **rova** period are made and administered by the chief and the headmen of all the clans in the village. The rules are not new as they are incorporated from a previous **rova** period. When such rules become ineffective they are altered to become lenient or more harsh. Following is the account of **rova** obtained from the chief and a number of clan headmen of Paramana village.

> The village chief appoints men from six different clans as **katimani** or policemen who are watchdogs. At the end of each day about six o'clock a conch shell is blown three times, warning gardeners and hunters to return home. The **katimani** at certain checkpoints check the people returning home. The people are checked as they may have restricted plant produce and garden crops in their possession. People found infringing the rule were reported to the village chief who indirectly enters into a "shouting and yelling match" with the assistance of other **katimani,** warning the wrongdoers that they were to be sanctioned according to the **rova** rules. Primarily, people are sanctioned by communal shame, intense gossiping, bad fortune or bad luck. Also, a huge traditionally-hollowed dish about 4 to 5 feet in length and two feet in width must be filled with important and prestigeous cooked food such as yam, bananas, taro and fish oiled with coconut milk.
>
> With these, a huge pig and bananas were to accompany two wrongdoers to the chief's house. To prepare for such an occasion was costly for a wrongdoer, therefore kinsmen also gave mutual aid and assistance in some form or another. The food was shared among the village people. Significant is the ideology of sanctioning the wrongdoer to suffer the social, political and economic constraints imposed upon him/her. Thus, this deters the wrongdoers from continuing the disapproved idea in the society and educates the potential wrongdoers.

Disputes Concerning Land and Women:

Problems over land and women were perceived by the people as serious matters. This is because land is associated with wealth, prestige and status. A person with considerable land had influence over people who become his followers and supporters. They need not have been his kinsmen, basically they become followers or supporters to acquire more land in the name of their leader. In doing so, the followers had other collective rights such as usufruct rights of land plants. A dispute with weak groups resulted in amalgamation that enlarges the control of the group.

Fights over women involved different villages of the Aroma coast. The memory cases I have elicited occured between Paramana and Maopa villages. In these traditional woman fights known as **veala,** both men and women are involved. The roles women play in **veala** were regulated by the customary rules of the fight. A woman followed her brother who fought with other men. When he was in trouble or was badly injured, his sister intervened to help prevent the opponents from demolishing him. The women could hit the opponent.

The "fight over a woman" involved men who simultaneously expressed their willingness to marry her. The person who got married to her first provoked the other parties to declare a **veala** fight. If the husband of the woman was killed by the opponent party, the woman was obtained by them. Fights over women lasted over a week, and involved allied villages, clans, and supporters. In these fights, old traditional rivals renewed their old fights over women and land. Because of the seriousness and importance of land and women, customary rules relating to marriage and land tenure and succession will be described in some detail.

MARRIAGE

The Paramana people use **kwalu** as the equivalent to the anthropological term "clan". Marriage in **kwalu** is exogamous and residence is patrilocal. **Kwalu** membership consists primarily of agnates, but there are other relatives, especially male and female affines, who renounce their affiliation with their natal **kwalu** and work and support the host group. Their rights over communal assets such as residential locality, garden land, canoes, fishing nets and ritual paraphernalia are equally as important as the rights of agnate members.

Three forms of marriage are monogamy, polygyny and capture. Monogamy, implicitly and explicitly, is the universal and approved form of marriage on the basis of Christian doctrines. The polygamous marriage is not common today. In the past, chiefs took advantage of their wealth to obtain women as wives. It was not only the chiefs who had the advantage, their supporters or followers with wealth such as land, gardens, pigs; and those recognised as industrious workers also had a number of wives. A number of wives meant a labour force that added to efficient economic advantage. Increase in the labour force resulted in an increase in produce that flourished in the chief's name. From reliable sources and observation in Paramana village, polygamous marriage was more commonly practised in last few decades than today.

Another common way of getting a wife was "capture" marriage. Patrol Reports evidently indicate that in the last two decades, capture marriage was a common way of marrying. Many informants during the period of this research were of the opinion that many capture marriages went unreported, as the offended groups were either too weak to retaliate or feared that if the kiap knew, they too were in strife. However, a few such marriages that came to the notice of the visiting Patrol Officer and other colonial administrators were intensely supressed and sanctioned. Following is the description of a capture marriage recited to me by Vagi, one of my informants.

> In any case, if initial stages of the negotiation between the boy's side and the girl's side fail, then the boy's side may resort to capture strategy. Despite the boy and girl not knowing each other as friends, if the boy indicate's his intention to his parents and kinsmen, capture strategy is perceived by the people as the best way. In the course of capturing the girl, the boy must force the girl to have sexual intercourse whilst onlookers watch. At a later date, if the girl runs away, they would be regarded as married. The girl is no longer a girl but known to the people as **kapani.** Until they rejoin, the name becomes detached and void. In most cases, girls rejoin their said husbands as social circumstances do not allow such behaviour.

Marrying ages vary from 17 to 25. Most boys and girls are betrothed by their parents. Parents of the boy or the girl choose who their child should marry. Young people who disapprove of their parents attitudes are forced to marry accordingly. Otherwise the parents would dislike the girl or boy their child chooses to marry, which means a boy who chooses his own wife will to a greater extent suffer social sanctions. Bride price payment will be delayed. "Delayed" marriages are due to absence from home, disruption of social status and difficulty in gathering bride exchange wealth (bride price payment). A number of men and women are bachelors and spinsters for life, because of mental delusion, deformed appearance and/or disrupted social status.

Marriage rules are determined by chosen social relationships. Marriage is exogamous in patrilineal clan descent. It is also considered exogamous in cognatic groups, for the reason that both patrilineal and matrilineal links are important. Social links breached in marriage are socially sanctioned by intense gossip, shame, and delay in bride wealth exchange. Thus the stigma of disrupting the social tie remains attached for a long time.

Marriage arrangements are organised by the cognatic kinsmen of both the bride and groom. Bride wealth exchange is dependent upon cognatic kinsmen who make a social investment on the consideration that they will be reimbursed on a similar occasion.

Premarital sexual intercourse is discouraged. A girl having an illegitimate child is ejected from the nuclear family for a lengthy period of time until the social disruption and shame done to the family's reputation is restored. The girl is sanctioned severely by gossip and shame. A number of cases revealed that parents apply violent physical punishment to their daughters. The stigma is attached for life to the illegitimate pregnancy and the child. An illegitimate child is thought of as someone having no place in the village and is regarded with contempt. Also the child may become a **bona fide** member of the father's group if the marriage is validated by customary exchanges and the child is adopted.

All illegitimacy cases are brought to the attention of the village people through intense gossiping and later become a serious matter for Councillors, village elders and Village Court officials to solve. The accused man is named by the pregnant woman as the cause of the pregnancy. He is ordered by the authoritarian agents to maintain the illegitimate child according to the customary rules, to adopt the child, or to validate their marriage. The named father puts aside a share of either cooked food or garden food for the child. When the mother receives the food, her duty is to tell the child that his/her father has sent them for him/her. The child learns who her/his father is, so at the time of adoption the father is not seen as a stranger. Illegitimate marriage can be validated only if the named man's side agrees. In doing so, reciprocal exchanges of food publicly indicate the union of the two. The support of the kinsmen motivate the man and woman to come together as husband and wife.

The payment of bride wealth exchanges rescinds any form of illegitimacy pregnancy and clears the disrupted social status of the two parties. The marriage is regarded as valid and the child becomes a legitimate child of the two. In cases where marriage negotiations fail, force is applied by the remedy agent for the couple to marry.

Residence after marriage is patrilocal. The married couple live with the husband's parents until a new house is erected. The children are domiciled with the parents in their natal clan, but are taught the consanguineal and affinal ties. Though they do not have any property rights in their matriline, they are obliged to know their basic matrilineal links since through this relationship they have loosely defined property rights in land and garden plots. Upon request or invitation, usage rights, especially to garden land, are extended for a garden season. This means they only have rights in crops they plant but not ownership to land.

Adultery is seen by Paramana people as a serious crime. Husbands and wives see each other as having exclusive sexual rights. A man having a love affair with another man's wife is violating his sexual rights. Violating a man's sexual rights is a grave insult. It is equally paired with killing the man. Not only is the aggrieved man deprived of his sexual rights, but his kinsmen are collectively drawn into the dispute as they also have some rights. The violated sexual rights affect all kinsmen who directly or indirectly support the man in assembling the bride wealth. Normally, the aggrieved party retaliates violently and the entire affair thus escalates into a big fight where supporters help each side. The oral evidence has shown from village informants that in the past, villages on the Aroma coast would fight a war over a woman, where supporters were drawn from different villages. These fights have ended up in either side loosing lives.

Where the fight is perceived as a bad strategy, intensive gossiping deters the parties to adultery. The gossiping does not reach the aggrieved party as the affair may develop into a fight. The Christian ideologies are emphasized and taught by Pastors and Reverends to suppress villagers in committing adultery. The Deacons and other Christian converts preach the subject to villagers that adultery is a sin and the penalty is hell. Despite speculation about discovering parties to adultery, very little is done to do justice to the aggrieved party's side. Usually it is ignored until the aggrieved party discovers and does justice to it. Most cases of adultery have been summoned to Reverends and Pastors who remedy the situation.

Adultery with unmarried girls is considered less serious. It may not be perceived as adultery, as the notion of polygamous marriage requires a man to court young suitable girls to be chosen as his wife or wives. The adulterer's wife knowing about the affair may result in an overt fight between the girl and the wife, this depends particularly on the control of the husband. Some men are authoritarian over their spouses and thus are suppressed from creating disputes. It seems married men courting unmarried girls is not regarded as an adultery act, but is seen together with the rules of the polygamous marriage.

There are a number of reasons why married couples divorce. Usually, husbands divorce their wives. A wife who runs away or departs from a husband is accused of having been seduced by another man. This involves serious clashes between the husband and wife so that the women conform to proper behaviour as married women. A wife who does not conform to the roles and rules of a married woman is likely to be divorced by the husband on the advice of the parents. A bad wife is one who does not respect and listen to her mother-in-law's advice, does little gardening and domestic work, and is seen behaving like a girl. She does not conform to certain restrictions as a married woman. Adultery is also a cause of divorce. Either one of the spouses involved in committing adultery makes the other repudiate the marriage.

When a marriage is repudiated, the wife returns back to her natal clan with her youngest children below the age of six. The families of the husband and wife enter into an avoidance relationship. The affinal relations end and supporters become enemies. However, because the father would have the custody of older children and the mother would have the custody of younger ones, there is freedom of children visiting both sides without intimidation from any side. On either side, the children are well looked after and cared for. Therefore, the father has more right on the custody of children. Because the mother gave birth to the children, she has the right of benefitting from the children's wealth when they grow older and go to school and are engaged in wage employment.

Divorce cases are considered private affairs between husband and wife. Thus it is not overtly declared, but the people learn from hearing and seeing parties in avoidance relationships.

LAND TENURE AND SUCCESSION

Today ownership of land is becoming increasingly important. The rapid population growth to 1,020 people today compared to 430 people in the 1930s has caused many people to demand their rightful pieces of land in which transfer of ownership was by gift through cognatic links. From a customary law of succession point of view, the land ownership passed through patrilineal links. Under such system, a wife is of little significance. A father's property, such as houses, canoes, fishing gear, dancing gear and land, on his decease, devolves to his sons, as illustrated in Figure 21.1.

In this sub-clan of Roagolo, Ulea's sons Iamo, Roae, Pepena and Gerega would succeed and inherit their father's property. Before their father dies, the land and property would be divided according to seniority in the line of brothers.

However, sometimes a proportion of the property and the land is transferred by way of gift or goodwill act from father to daughter. In this case the land had passed from Ulea to his daughter Thoa to her sons and daughters after she had died. The ownership of this type of land is under question by the males in direct line. This is because land is valued as a scare resource and important property.

There are two types of land in Paramana. First is the one identified with cemetaries and regarded as ancestoral grounds. This type of land is

Figure 21.1

SUB–CLAN OF ROAGOLO.

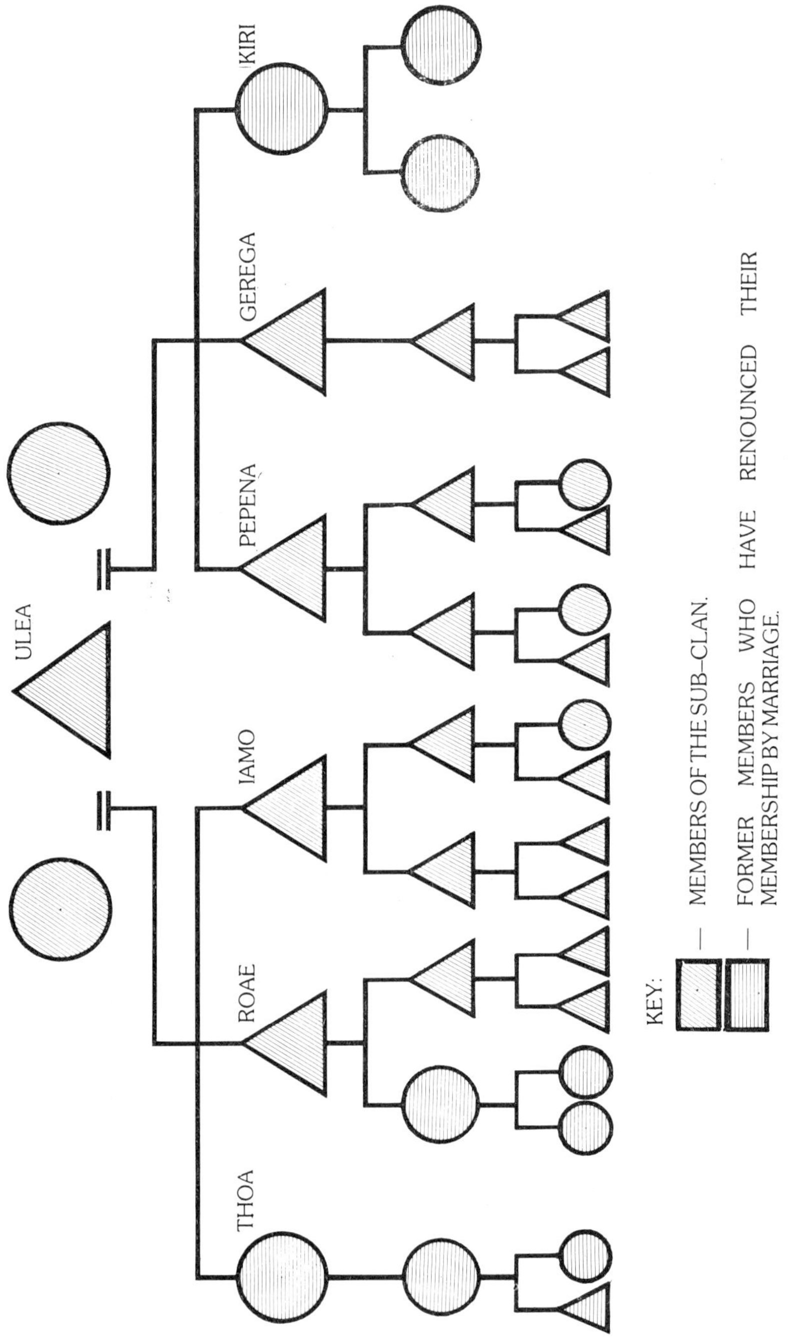

predominantly covered with coconut groves, betelnut palms, edible fruit trees (i.e. mangoes, castard apples etc.) banana trees and the like. Each lineage has its own burial grounds. Ritual ceremonies associated with garden magic are performed on this site. The dead ancestors and kinsmen are named and called upon to make the gardens, coconuts, betelnuts, bananas, etc. flourish and the year be a fruitful one.

The general customary rule of succession is son to succeed father to land property. Thus Ulea in Figure 21.1 will be succeeded by the eldest son Iamo. Iamo will inherit all the important material property and important gardening sites and ceremonial land. However, the less important but still significant wealth will pass to three other sons Roae, Pepena and Gerega. Although the divided proportions of land are owned by the four sons of Ulea, the property rights are vested in all the kinsmen. This means the two sisters Thoa and Kiri have the right to obtain coconuts, betelnuts and the like. Likewise the four sons share property rights in freely obtaining such property as betelnuts, coconuts and bananas from each other's gardens. These harvesting rights are misinterpreted by many women who have married out of their clans and think that they have land.

Secondly, garden land ownership is vested in the head of the sub-clan. Figure 21.1 indicates that Iamo is headman, so the ownership to all the important gardening sites is vested in him. Other small patches are held under the exclusive right to invite others to use the land. The important land, whose ownership is held by the headman, is communal land. Every sub-clan member has the right to use it and to invite other kinsmen to make gardens and enjoy it. It is difficult to transfer ownership by sale or lease because every clan member having some right must consent to such a tranfer or ownership.

There are no individual rights to a garden plot. As the land is cleared for garden purposes, the headman with the assistance of this wife allocates a plot to individual families in the sub-clan. The task of allocating plots is also done by individual families who initiate the cleaning site of a garden. It does not have to be the headman and his wife only. Hunting and fishing are village affairs. No one individual owns the pigs and wallabies in the bush or fish in the waters or reefs. Therefore, fishing and hunting grounds are communually owned by the entire village.

Most disputes have occurred as a result of infringing on land boundaries. The land or garden boundaries are symbolized by certain plants planted by ancestors as markers. In some cases, deep drains are dug to distinctly mark garden boundaries between clans on sub-clan boundaries.

The corporate kin groups have defended their claim to boundary infringement by traditional markers. Working beyond one's lawful boundaries arouses tensions and disputes among groups. Land disputes start in this manner and escalate into fights. The strongest groups obtain such land by coercion and force other groups out.

Land disputes amongst villages of Aroma were common. In the past, more than sixty years ago, force and self-help were the main factors in deciding the ownership of disputed land. The introduction of Village Courts, land adjudicators, and remedy agents such as Councillors, Pastors and Patrol Officers have implanted court-like procedures where a Councillor or other big man presides to hear land dispute cases. The procedures and processes are rather like custom-dictated machinery which provides orderly procedures for detecting infringements and resolving disputes. In such courts, tracing kinship genealogies was an important aspect of knowing how the land had passed through various links over the years.

Consequently, the ownership of land is decided by the type of social system the people have. Land is transmitted through bilateral links either through the patriline, matriline, or through cognatic links depending on the type of kinship structure. Thus, tracing these links is significant at court to establish before the audience and the third party as to how the land has devolved.

KIRIWINA (TROBRIAND ISLANDS)

MILNE BAY PROVINCE

Daniel Mark

INTRODUCTION

My research concentrated on two field sites, Gumilababa Village and Ilalima Village, which have differences in social organization patterns. Gumilababa Village is situated along the north coast road about 2.7 km from the District Headquarters at Losuia. It is one of the most important coastal villages with a population of about 400-500 people, and is the traditional residence place of the chiefs who control the Kuboma Sector of the Trobriand Islands. The present chief, Chief Pulitala, resides there now. Chiefs exercise absolute power in Kiriwina unlike big men in many parts of Papua New Guinea. Although most of my contacts in Gumilababa were commoners, the chief was an important informant.

Ilalima Village is contrasted with Gumilababa in that it is a small village situated along the east coast road and about 9 km from Losuia. The population is about 200 people. The village is not clustered in one place, but consists of separate homestead areas with short distances separating them. Although the village has a chief, he does not exercise absolute power as in Gumilababa. The headman, a commoner, is a renowned gardener who exercises control in some parts of the village. He has been my contact and informant.

Table 22.1 presents a summary of categories of customary law in Kiriwina. For the balance of this report, I will discuss each of these categories in turn, summarizing the principles of customary law.

Table 22.1

SUBSTANTIVE LAW OUTLINE

KIRIWINA (MILNE BAY PROVINCE)

BREACHES OF CUSTOMARY LAW

1. Land ownership
2. Disputes over women (adultery, mistreatment of women)
3. Theft of garden produce, fruit trees, animals and other properties
4. Inheritance and succession
5. Sorcery
6. Non-performance of traditional obligations

INTERPERSONAL CONFLICTS

1. Disputes over girls (sexual rivalries)
   (a) between members of same village
   (b) between members of different villages

2. Domestic Arguments
   (a) within the clan or lineage
   (b) between different clans or lineages

3. **Bulitilaula:** a competition in which rivals compete with their wealth, especially long yams, in order to shame their opponent as a means of gaining prestige by displaying yams.

4. Conflict over domestic animals

LAND OWNERSHIP

The following principles of land ownership have been taken from interviews regarding matters on land. Firstly, land is communally owned by a clan, subclan or lineage in which a senior active member is or acts as trustee. He is responsible for allocating and distributing land to members of the clan or lineage and to other persons (payment made in traditional money or cash) for gathering purposes or otherwise. Land is inalienable, except in cases where land had been used as compensation for death, or in rare cases where no heir exists to inherit the land. In some cases, the children of the "trustee" enjoy the privilege of using the land without payment. This privilege ceases at the death of the trustee. In such cases, in order to keep good relations among the trustee's children and lineages or clan, payment in the form of money or a feast is performed or paid to the trustee's children by the lineage of the trustee. This completes the return of property. Finally, dispositions and remedies used in land disputes depend upon the relatives statuses of the litigants.

DISPUTES OVER WOMEN

Adultery:

This is a frequent factor which raises conflicts and is a serious crime in customary law. Trespass of sexual rights is punishable according to the circumstances of the case. In principle, redress for trespass of sexual rights includes physical violence, break-up of marriages, yam competition, and finally sorcery. However, redress and disposition depend upon the economic, political or sorcery power and status of the parties. Adultery by a man of high status with the wife of a person of low status is not serious. In such cases, the complainant or his relatives send the woman away, possibly after physical harm. However if it is opposite, the complainant is in a strong position to use the punishment mentioned above to punish the adulterer. In many adultery cases, physical violence is not resorted to except as regards the wife. Sorcery is relied on to punish the male wrongdoer.

Mistreatment of Women:

Mistreatment of women is tolerable as it is regarded as a matter between spouses. Interference by a lineage may disturb the relationship between the spouses' lineages. However this tolerance is rescinded if the mistreatment is too frequent and if insulting words are used as regards the wife's lineages. (See Case 1505). The wife's lineage may punish the husband by forcing the daughter to leave him, or in extreme cases, may use physical violence or yam competition to degrade him. Finally, the relative statuses of the litigants have an impact on dispositions and remedies resorted to.

THEFT OF GARDEN PRODUCE AND PROPERTY

Theft of garden produce and fruit trees is a common crime. However the disposition in regard to punishment consists mainly of psychological remedies (such as public shaming) and reliance on supernatural or divine beings for punishing offenders. The use of certain signs symbolizing ownership and preventing access is thought to result in certain divine punishment if breached. It is considered, in this case, to be inviting sorcery retaliation and therefore, no payments are demanded by aggrieved parties as observed in my survey.

In other cases, such as the theft of a canoe, claims for compensation are considered only when the property has been damaged or lost by the offender who took the property without permission of the owner. However, in a case where a canoe is taken with the intent to deprive the owner of his property, return of the canoe is effected if the canoe is recovered, and the offender is further punished by public shaming.

In the case of a pig theft, similar patterns apply. That is, the pig is returned if it is discovered undamaged. Otherwise, compensation is asked for. Killing a pig in one's own garden is justified. It is at the discretion of the pig owner to seek compensation by letting the killer have the meat and pay some compensation in return. If the pig owner keeps the meat, the killer is free from any obligation for the death of the pig. Of course, in all the cases, the disposition and remedies for conflicts depend upon the relative statuses of the litigants and the circumstances in which the property is taken.

INHERITANCE AND SUCCESSION

Customary law divides principles of inheritance and succession to property into two parts. Inheritance of communally-owned property which is strictly passed on through the matrilineal line, and alienable property generally passed on to children of the lineage. Firstly, communally-owned property and some sorcery knowledge passes through the matrilineal line automatically by accepted rule. Generally a male elder member acts as trustee; however, where there is no appropriate male member, females are in a position to inherit the property. In the second case, property may be alienated to another member of the lineage who pays or renders shell money or services to the lineage property owner. The process is known as **pokala** ("tax", however not compulsory). In payment, the person paying **pokala** is rewarded with the property.

SORCERY

The institution of sorcery is very important in the life of the Trobriands. It is usually classified as a beneficial activity concerned with curing; helping to bring luck; making food grow; or bringing fish, rain and sun when needed. Sorcery is monopolised by only a few people, therefore only a certain segment of the community knows or uses sorcery for benefit or destruction. Thus people pay for the services of sorcerers. Sorcery knowledge is passed on within the lineage for fear of reprisal if the knowledge is passed on to other lineages. I was told that the source of power and status in a village depends upon sorcery power as well as economic and political power.

In customary law, destructive sorcery is a serious crime and punishment is usually killing. Nowadays, indirect killing by using sorcery against sorcery is a remedy. Thus sorcery can be used as punishment as well as being a crime.

TRADITIONAL EXCHANGES

Traditional exchanges place an important obligation on contracting parties. Contracting parties exchange not only material goods, but also relations. Failure to fulfil the obligation affects both these relationships and the reputation of contracting parties. In some cases, force can be used to get what the other is obliged to give. The parties not fulfilling obligations suffer as the other party shames them. This may result in further exchanges. Thus, in the case of non performance of traditional obligations, consequences are grave, and physical violence or sorcery may be resorted to as disposition remedies.

SEXUAL RIVALRIES

Girls (sometimes even boys) are considered as the "sole property" of the village. Consequently, a man courting a girl from another village is likely to be physically assaulted if caught. Many of the open conflicts between villages are rooted in such assaults. The relative statuses of the parties is an important factor in the disposition of such conflicts, and in grave cases, the whole village may become involved. The village chief has the final say in any conflict arising between villages, and therefore his decision is the law, but most cases are settled through consensus. Compensations are awarded and payments for keeping the injured are made.

DOMESTIC ARGUMENTS

An argument between lineages is an affair for the lineages to settle and the community does not take part. In such arguments, matters are settled immediately, whether by consensus or by other means. Conflicts between different lineages are much more serious. In such cases, the disposition differs depending upon the nature of the conflict. Settlement is usually difficult. However, the chief is responsible for bringing both parties to compromise. Relative and economic status are taken into account in the final disposition. Where one party is not satisfied with the settlement, sorcery may be resorted to.

CONFLICTS OVER ANIMALS (other than pigs)

Conflicts over animals is settled through consensus. Compensation is paid, the amount depending upon the relative statuses of litigants. Because animals are not valued, conflicts are minimal. Litigants fear ridicule if the conflict escalates too far, resulting in extreme modes of dispute settling such as physical violence or a yam dispute.

CHIEFS

The chiefs have a very powerful position in Kiriwina. A chief (together with elders) forms a legislature. A chief is a judge as well and his decision regarding any village affairs is final. In cases where land has no inheritor, the chief automatically owns the land and signifies his power. Though the chief's word is law, he always consults the elders of the village before making decisions.

UBIRI

ORO PROVINCE

Marcel Dixon Mes

INTRODUCTION

This research was conducted between November 1979 and February 1980 in the Wanigela region. Wanigela is situated in the Collingwood Bay area of the Northern (Oro) Province and lies far east or south-east from the Provincial Capital Popondetta towards the border between Northern and Milne Bay Provinces. Wanigela itself has a population of 800-1,000 people or more. Basically, the population is made up of the three major language groups: the Ubiri people, the Maniorot people and the Onjob/Isor people. The present research only dealt with the customary laws of the Ubiri people and not the other two groups. Research methods consisted of extended case collection and in the form of interviews and "story telling" involving both elderly people and younger adults who have had some form of formal education.

Table 23.1 gives a summary of categories of customary law among the Ubiri people. Each category will be discussed in turn.

Table 23.1

CATEGORIES OF UBIRI CUSTOMARY LAW

CUSTOMARY LAWS CONCERNING LAND

1. Ownership of land
2. Land tenure
3. Inheritance and succession to land
4. Disputes and settlements regarding land

INHERITANCE OF PROPERTY AND CEREMONIAL RITES

1. Property inheritance
2. Ceremonial rights, inheritance or succession

THEFT OF GARDEN PRODUCE AND OTHER PRODUCTS

INTERPERSONAL CONFLICT

1. Mistreatment of women
2. Adultery

BREACHES OF OTHER CUSTOMARY LAW

1. Entry into an area or village with intention to fight
2. Disputes and settlement
3. Fighting
4. Crimes against a person (false accusation, defamation, rape, etc.)

CUSTOMARY LAWS CONCERNING LAND

Ownership of Land:

Land is considered as the most valuable property in Ubiri society. Because a lot of importance is attached to it, it would be very difficult to have individual ownership. Apart from the above reason, social organization is based on a clan system. Thus it is very clear that land is communally owned by groups, usually clans. This pattern of ownership would be found in areas surrounding the village, in other words, areas where there is much gardening activity, hunting, fishing or where raw materials are acquired. Most of the clans would own land around the vicinity of village activity.

However, land that is not particularly owned by any clan, is or was tribal or society owned. The main reason was that the clans joined together as one people, one force, and defended such territories against aggressors. This sort of land is probably what is now known as crown land. Thus, land is clan-owned, that is, the immediate territory surrounding the village activity area. Land that is village-owned, or common land, is land beyond the customary clan land.

Land Tenure:

Land is considered free for use for normal gardening purposes. Anyone from any clan can garden on any part of the customarily-owned lands. Apart from gardening, raw material is also free for use. Hunting and fishing was free. This was normally allowed because it did not mean permanent ownership of the land.

However, customary restrictions were evident if people from other clans wanted to plant crops like sago, coconuts, betelnuts and cash crops that may be permanent. Thus, permissable use of land that belonged to another clan only involved short-term crops or purposes; that is, mainly for gardening food crops, hunting and for collecting materials. Land outside the clan-owned boundaries was and is available for public use.

People who were in the clan had the right and freedom to use whatever their clan owned. However, in a clan system, one can always find the "seniors" or the customarily recognised families and the others, the "juniors", who make up the clan. For permanent land use, for example planting coconuts or cash crops, it was customary for consultation with "seniors" to take place before anything was done in order to avoid conflict.

Inheritance and Succession:

In almost all cases, offspring born within the clan have the right to succeed to property rights of their fathers. However, there are particular or rare cases where land can be inherited or succeeded to by members of other clans. Example of such cases follow:

Example 1

Where a particular clan (A) backs up another clan (B) in their dispute with yet another clan (C) over land: Because members of clan A received "blood" or even "death", B has an **obligation** to pay compensation for the support it has had from clan A, especially if there are casualties from clan A. In such situations, a piece of land (i.e. from clan B) may be part of the payment to clan A. Such is customary. In some cases, land may be inherited by clan A from clan B either for permanent or short term use. However, in nearly all cases, all the land rights of that particular plot of land would be transferred from B to A. Thus, clan A is now the rightful owner of that particular piece of land, but no more than that within the boundary that is put down by clan B.

Example 2

Where a child is adopted by another clan because his whole clan has been wiped out for some reason or other: The particular clan responsible for looking after the child take into custody all the property that he or she or their clan may have owned. After he or she reaches maturity, all the rights of the property should be returned to him or her and any offspring.

Example 3

Where a female member of the clan marries into another clan: If she is the eldest, she may be given a piece of land that she and her husband may use throughout their lifetime. If she dies, the property is automatically returned to her birthright clan. In some cases, her offspring may make use of the property on the land, e.g. betelnuts, but cannot own the land.

Example 4

Where a respected figure (example, the eldest of the chiefs) dies or is killed by enemies at a particular location: The clan that owns the land may give that part of the land away to the descendants of the deceased. It is then inherited by the new owners and the former owners have nothing to do with it anymore.

Example 5

Where an individual from one clan or area is adopted into another clan: That individual has the right to garden or collect raw materials from the territory of his adopted clan. However, he has no birthright ownership of that land, and therefore, he cannot succeed his father, even if his father is the eldest in the clan. He will have to have the approval of the birthright clan members before he can do anything permanent on the land.

These are some of the principles involving inheritance and succession to land. Land is considered to be so important an asset that inheritance and succession to land has its own rules and regulations. It is solely up to the clan concerned whether any land right gifts be permanent or on a "loan" basis, depending on the circumstances. However, land is inherited and succeeded to by offspring who are born as members of the clan, especially male members. Females may inherit temporarily, but because they will marry outside the clan they have limited rights.

Disputes and Settlement Regarding Land:

There are many reasons why disputes may arise over land, and it is quite easy to see how or why they arise. Here I will discuss how settlements of such disputes come about. In all cases, if the matter concerns a land case, a meeting is called by either of the disputing parties. All the elders of the village as well as the village people attend such a meeting. The way the dispute is solved is by oral history. Most of the clans know their landmarks and their oral history (passed down by word of mouth). Thus, at the meeting, oral history of the landmarks and ownership is discussed by several elders or other knowledgeable individuals. From such oral history, people realize who the rightful owner is and agree that the stories are true, or if most of the knowledgeable people tell a similar story, then the disputing parties know who the rightful owner of the land is and land marks and boundaries are clarified. The basic idea is that land disputes are thrown out in the open where the experts put their knowledge together. Where most of the people agree that the oral history is familiar to them, that is the story their fathers passed on to them, then it is clear who becomes the winner and loser of the case.

INHERITANCE OF PROPERTY AND CEREMONIAL RIGHTS

Property:

It is customary that any property that belongs to the father individually will automatically be inherited by his immediate sons and daughters. This property includes betelnut trees, sago and coconuts as well as other plants. On the other hand, if he has adopted a son or a daughter (that is, if he has none of his own), they too have the right to such property. However, if he has no offspring, then his property can be inherited by his next of kin, his brother. If there is no brother, then the ownership goes to a member of the clan which the deceased had chosen before he died. In such a case where the property is given to a cousin or next of kin from another clan for some reason or other, then they have the right to own the property but not the land.

Land is one particular property that is not individually owned, however. One has a birth right inheritance to the clan-owned land which permits participation in communal ownership. However, nowadays, because of the existence of plantations that individuals may own on clan land, it seems there is individual ownership of that part of clan land.

Ceremonial Rights:

Each patrilineal clan has its own form of decorations, designs, paintings, etc. according to their totems. Every member born automatically inherits such ceremonial rights. However, there are a few exceptions. By our custom, the first born in each family is normally initiated. At this initiation ceremony, it is customary that the mother's brothers decorate the offspring and transmit the ceremonial rights of the mother's clan. This is conducted in a public ceremony so that everyone in the village realises that the particular individual, although from another clan, is also part of the mother's clan. Thus, he and he alone is able to use both his mother's and father's customary ceremonial rights. In other words, his younger brothers or sisters cannot use such symbols; even his own children can't use them. When he dies, the ceremonial rights return to the place of origin. Thus, it is only under special circumstances that members of one clan may use ceremonial rights belonging to another, (i.e. if they have birthrights in both groups). Generally speaking, inheritance of physical property or ceremonial rights is patrilineal, passing on through the father's clan.

THEFT OF GARDEN PRODUCE AND OTHER PRODUCTS

Stealing and destruction of property are regarded as degrading conduct. Such actions can lead to fighting or even death through sorcery if no compensation payment is made. However, the severity of the case or the action taken depends on the value that people place on the property in question and on the relative inappropriateness of the actions.

In the case of garden theft, the offender is generally accused with strong words intended to shame the thief. If the owner catches the offender "red-handed", he can either take back the property, fight with the offender on the spot, or allow the thief to have the stolen property but also give a warning. Another possibility is for the owner to let the thief go without making his presence known, and then remove him if he is a sorcerer, or bring the matter out in public on return to the village. If, on the other hand the incident is witnessed and reported by a person other than the owner, the matter is often dealt with in public. In such case, the owner of the garden may go to the residence of the offender and accuse him of the theft, making it possible for the public to witness the whole incident.

In the case of simple garden theft, most of the informants indicated that very little compensation is actually paid. Depending on the individuals concerned, the event is normally just forgotten. If any payment is to be made it is often made in secret. Payment usually takes place if the matter has not been thrown out into the public. Payment can be made in terms of the amount of food stolen, plus some pig meat etc., as long as the total amount is a little bit more than what was stolen, so that the wounds are completely healed.

Other products including sago, pigs, chickens, and dogs have greater value to the people. If such products are stolen, and enquiries reveal that the persons concerned are known, there is bound to be trouble unless something is done. It is important to point out that, in most cases, the owner gives the people concerned time to appear before bringing the matter up in public. Normally, the thieves are made aware of the fact that the owner of the property knows about the incident. Thus the responsible party enlists the help of his immediate family or even clan members to help to pay for the compensation. This compensation is made secretly without the knowledge of the public.

Compensation payment is made in terms of either returning exactly what was stolen, providing a similar object, or by paying with shells or ornaments. The rule of customary law is that the value paid must equal the worth of the property stolen. However, in most cases, a little extra was also paid in order to clear everything off.

A suprising thing concerning compensation is the fact that the judgement on how much to pay is made by the person who stole the property. However, if the victim feels that the payment is not worth as much as his or her property, then by customary terms he or she has the right to complain and ask for a bit more which of course will be paid. Equiries revealed that somehow or other, the people roughly know the worth of the property concerned. Compensation payments, however, are established depending on the worth of the objects as well as to create a much more friendly atmosphere between the parties concerned.

INTERPERSONAL CONFLICTS

Mistreatment of Women:

There are customary limits to the mistreatment of women by their husbands even though it may be a domestic problem. Customary law allows for some form of punishment or control for such actions. While taking into account the private nature of the dispute, excessiveness as well as frequency of abuse are considered. Customary law also allows for the fact that if the woman feels that she has been unjustly victimised, she can pack up and take refuge with her brothers or clansmen. This of course is generally temporary, although she can stay as long as she likes depending on the individual's temperament and the seriousness of the mistreatment. The penalty is that the man is left alone, and of course is deprived of the comforts of his wife. There is also indirect pressure put on him from the community who may have witnessed the episode or is talking about it.

Another section in this sort of law allows for the brothers of the woman to rescue her. That is to say that the brothers, after assessing the situation, have the right to take their sister away from her husband. The brothers may even challenge their brother-in-law if the events are serious and if they think that the woman concerned is unjustly mistreated. She can remain with her brothers until such time that they see fit that their sister should return to her husband.

However, when the sister is returned, it is customary that she returns with presents, especially food and pigs. This of course "symbolises" the fact that the relationship is normalised again and the "wounds are healed". Thus taking away the woman, depriving the husband of the comforts of his wife for a period, challenges from the woman's brothers and indirect pressure from the community all contribute to the penalty of the man who mistreats his wife.

Adultery:

This offence is considered by customary law to be one of the most serious and complex problems to solve. Offences include making approaches or signs, going after the woman, and making attempts as well as the actual act. Such incidents can be brought to the husband's or wife's attention depending on who is involved. However, the severity of the case depends on the parties involved. For example, a married man involved with a single woman is not as serious as a married man involved with a married woman or even a married woman with a single man. The latter two are much more serious simply because it involves a man's wife. All in all, adultery cases are serious and the consequences are great.

In the case of a married man involved with a single woman, when such an incident is brought to the notice of the wife, the only thing the wife can do is to beat up that woman. This is considered to be normal by the people. It is "customary law" that at such times, she with the aid of her friends or sisters can challenge the woman who has been "stealing" her husband. The trouble-maker also has the right to defend herself, though at times she may not be aided by her friends or sisters. The incident is thrown out into the public and the public also has a say in the matter. There is no formal settlement or peace gathering for such incidents except that the other parties may get involved in trying to solve the issue.

Customary law considers the case of a married man involved with a married woman to be more serious than the above case. When such an incident is brought to the notice of the husband, he can do several things. Without making any fuss he can kill his enemy through sorcery. In other words, death is one alternative, and customary law allows for this. Normally, however, if the woman responded to the man, and adultery was actually committed, the husband has a right to beat up the woman instead of going after the man concerned. If on the other hand, if the wife did not respond to the approaches, the husband still has the right to challenge the man who made the approaches. When the husband challenges such a man, there is no warning to his enemy. In such cases, customary law allows "striking first before talking", so the husband strikes at his opponent as soon as the opponent is in view.

When the husband concerned enters the other man's hamlet, his brothers or clansmen have every right to back him up. Likewise the accused can also have people from his side to back him up, if he had warned them that something of this nature was coming up. The plaintiff should attack no one but the accused, and the plaintiff's clansmen are on standby to fight with the accused's clansmen who might like to challenge the plaintiff's people.

According to customary law, the accused must tolerate a certain amount of punishment before he can strike back. That is to say that after repelling the enemy's blows five or six times, then he is in a position to strike back in order to defend himself. In most cases, such incidents develop into big fights and sometimes involve bloodshed. Fights are stopped by other clans; parties who are not directly involved in the conflict. For adultery cases, it is important to point out that there are no peace ceremonies between the clans concerned. The incident is just forgotten over time by the individuals not directly involved in the adultery case. As for the individuals who are directly involved, informants mentioned that the ill feelings will remain as long as they live. Adultery cases are complex issues and cannot be easily solved.

BREACHES OF OTHER CUSTOMARY LAWS

Entry into an Area or Village with Intention to Fight:

People interviewed mentioned that under customary law anyone who enters another village is liable to be challenged. Information reveals that in solving conflicts whether small or large, entering someone else's area has to be treated with caution and respect. Even in attempting to solve a small conflict, one has to enter unarmed and in a peaceful manner. If one enters aggressively, the other party has no alternative but to meet them aggressively in order to defend their pride, and the reputation of the village. Though the people who defend the dignity of their village may be the trouble-makers in the first place, they will fight if one enters aggressively simply because they are defending their village, not because they want to defend their wrong-doings. Thus, to solve a problem, one has to enter peacefully.

Disputes and Settlement:

Domestic and individual disputes are normally settled with the particular individual (s) concerned. However, if it involves several clans, other measures are necessary depending on what the dispute is about. Traditionally, if various clans are involved in a fight, the chiefs of the village have the right to step in and help solve the problem. In other words if the situation affected the well-being of his community, the chief was the appropriate authority to solve the dispute.

Informants mentioned that if the chief commanded the disputing party to lay down their arms, it was automatically done. Nobody challenged his authority, unless of course he or she wanted to die through sorcery. Then through mediation in the form of discussions and concessions, the disputing parties agreed to a settlement. Peace ceremonies were then arranged where exchanges of food and goods took place between the two groups so the relationships were normalised again.

Fighting:

Though fighting is regarded as the normal thing to do before talking, it also has its rules. Within the village, people could get involved in a fight using clubs, but should only use that part of the club which might cause injury but not death. Killing was reserved for foreign enemies.

It is customary that where another group or groups, clan or individuals, aid an original party in a fight over land, women, etc.; rules also must apply to parties giving aid. Parties not directly involved are there for backup support. Normally, such parties become involved if the opposing party attacks or challenges them or when the party they come to aid is in a serious situation and in need of help. In the case where the members of one clan aid another clan, and as a result receive injuries, they are entitled to compensation from the clan they supported. For instance, in a case involving land, the clan responsible might give away part of the land either for temporary or permanent use. Otherwise, in a relatively minor case, a feast was provided where food and presents were given. If the dispute was over women or other similar matters, the clan responsible would put up a feast in their allies' honour, and food and presents would be given to them. As for the opposing parties, after reaching agreement, the groups exchange food and presents and even some important or valued objects to normalise the situation again.

Crimes Against a Person (False Accusation, Defamation, Rape, etc.):

Customary laws greatly emphasise the fact that people must have respect for each other. This is evident in the way in which justice is carried out against those who commit such crimes. if a person learns that false accusation or defamation has been laid upon him, he has no alternatives but to look for means and ways in which to clear his name. This of course means that the individual can act in various ways. The more common act would be to bring the matter to the notice of the community through a public challenge. This includes accusing the person of committing such crimes as well as fighting. Another alternative is to remove his opponent through sorcery, which is less common for ordinary people. The nature of the action taken depends very much on the nature of the individual and how he might take the insult, as well as the amount of damage done to him and his kinsmen and family.

Rape is a case which occurs only rarely. It is considered as an immoral and abnormal act, therefore people who commit such crimes are seen as very low in importance as human beings. Justice is accomplised through fighting. The victim's relatives have every customary right to challenge the offender and his supporters and to fight them whatever the cost. Apart from the actual physical challenge, the issue of the crime is exposed to the community. Public awareness and condemnation is in itself enough to punish any offender.

CONCLUSION

Customary laws discussed are what I consider to be major laws or practices. It is worth pointing out that our customary law relies heavily on fighting and challenging opponents in public places before settling down to solve the problem. It emphasises the notion that there is always time to normalise relationships and create a friendly atmosphere through exchanges of food, meat, presents, tobacco, etc., after challenging those who committed crimes. However, such exchanges also depended very much on the sort of crime committed. Adultery, for example, had no settlement except through fighting or death through sorcery. This seem to reflect the importance that people attached to a "man's wife" because of other cultural beliefs associated with wives and probably the life of the husband.

I have not considered or discussed minor cases in this project since such cases were either solved through talking and discussions under friendly terms or were simply forgotten because they were not worth the time and effort. The only form of justice was in the form of moral judgement and the people's opinion of the person concerned.

However, whichever way customary law deals with certain problems or crimes, it allows for justice to be done, and discourages crimes being committed. The fact is that customary law was based on the people's customary values in terms of respect for property and person and upon traditional values for harmonious living and for the survival and well being of the community. It is my belief that upon such values, customary law has been based and gradually shaped and molded into its present form.

HUNJARA

ORO PROVINCE

Nicodemus Araho

INTRODUCTION

In the Hunjara speaking area of Kokoda, stealing involves the removal of any type of property belonging to someone else without permission. For example, it may involve the removal of pigs, garden crops, clothes, weapons and tools, fruits from trees, or fishing and hunting in someone's area. I do not intend to cover all these types of theft, but rather will focus my attention on two contrasting cases, namely, stealing of a pig and stealing of taros in the garden. While stealing in any form is abhorred, it is the value of the stolen thing that the people take into account in judging the relative severity of the act.

Pig Stealing:

In my society, the value of pigs is very high due to a number of reasons. First, pigs are a symbol of wealth, and so the more pigs you have, the more wealthy you are. Therefore pigs bring power and prestige, and a man with many pigs is regarded as a hard-working man. As a result, when a pig is stolen it is no light matter. When the culprit is found, he must pay the owner a pig the same size as the one that was stolen. If he is reluctant to do so, the owner can spear a pig from the culprit's pen as payback for the loss of his own pig. However, if one is not available, then a piglet has to be obtained somehow and fed so that when it is big enough, it can be given to the owner of the stolen pig, However, at times the solution is not as easy as it seems since the thief may even deny having stolen the pig. This then results in the only alternative left, physical confrontation which may involve the use of spears and axes (with intent to severely injure or kill) or the use of bare hands (indicating need for less serious retaliation).

Taro Stealing:

Stealing of taro in its own right is a serious offence. However, the value of taro is lower than the value of pigs because while taro is plentiful and fairly easy to grow, pigs are hard to find and demand a lot of attention. There are certain ways of punishing culprits who steal taro.

The first method is that if the culprit is not found, then the owner of the stolen crop can gather the skins and the stalks of the taro (or any garden crop for that matter) and tie this onto a pole. The pole is then implanted on a public road so that the thief can be shamed when he sees the pole with the remains of the stolen crop as he or she passes by.

Secondly if the thief is known, a public announcement can be made in the village, thus punishing the thief through shame. However, more often than not the thief gets up to defend himself/herself which leads to verbal arguments. This at times leads to fights where relatives of both parties take sides to support their line.

Thirdly the thief can make a payment by giving back the amount of crops he had stolen to the owner. However, this type of action is very rare because word can get around that payment is being made for the theft of food crops from someone else's garden, thus shaming the thief further.

SHAME AS A REMEDY AGENT

Shaming is a technique for conflict management which is used as a means to publicly identify a trouble maker so that with this experience in mind, he or she won't be tempted to repeat a wrongful action again. It is a commonly used practice because it does not involve the use of dangerous weapons like spears and axes, which often are used to seriously injure or kill. However, the technique of shaming is not confined to one area alone, but there are many situations in which it can be used to achieve results. Some examples of these are shaming (of elders) due to disrespect, catching someone in a wrongful act (stealing, adultery, gossiping, etc.), wrongful accusations and so on. Some of the varied uses of shaming as a conflict reducing technique are illustrated by the following cases:

Case 1

In this case, X. enters Y.'s garden to assess the damage done to Y.'s garden by his pigs, so that he can repay Y. the amount equivalent to what was damaged. However upon learning of this, Y. views the action rather suspiciously and asks for an explanation for this type of action because in the first place no permission was obtained and secondly customary law dictates that no one should enter anybody's gardens or for that matter intrude into someone else's area. As a result, X. is shamed because of his actions which have been made public. However to show the purity of his intentions as well as to clear his name, he makes a feast and also presents a pig to Y. They then shake hands and apologise for their actions so that normal relationships can be continued.

Paying of respect to elders, parents or anybody regarded as senior because of their age is very important in maintaining harmonious relationships in the community. As it is, shame can occur through disrespect to senior members of the family or clan or any other institution for that matter. This type of action usually has a motive behind it, where junior members used disrespect to shame their seniors in certain situations.

Case 2

A senior member of the clan, man A., spears a pig belonging to man B., a junior member of the clan. B then feels very upset about the incident because great value is attached to the pig, and to feed another one is hard work. However as A. is an important man he cannot do anything but keep silent about the incident. The next day A. comes to apologise for his actions, but B. is not in the mood to accept apologies. Instead he goes into his house and shuts the door in A.'s face. Thus he shames A., obviously through the use of disrespect.

Case 3

In other cases X. insults Y. by saying that he is a lazy and unproductive man, never working in this garden but eating and sleeping all day. To prove him wrong, Y. works hard in his gardens and feeds pigs. When he is ready, he makes a big feast to the man who insulted him. X. is suprised but cannot refuse the feast. Instead he feels ashamed and also knows that he has a great debt to pay, in that he has to make a feast for Y. in payment for the one made to him.

INHERITANCÉ AND OWNERSHIP OF LAND

In most cases, land ownership is confined to clans rather than having individuals owning them as individual plots. This means that the right to use land is determined by being a member of a clan. As a result, young children who are born into the clan automatically become members of the clan and grow up knowing the rules and regulations of land use that safeguard proper use and administration of land.

In my society, customary law dictates that males must be given the first priority in the association of land and the resources on it. As a result, the first male that is born into the family automatically becomes the future head of the family's land and property. Any other male that is born into the family is subject to him. Although members of the family are allowed to use the land, it is present in the minds of each one that their elder brother is the head. However if no boys are born into the family then the father can do two things: let one of his daughters take charge of all the property and land, or find somebody else (preferably a male relative) to inherit his possession. In the former case, the woman then is rightly the owner of the possession and can use the land after she marries. Unlike other societies, she cannot be forced out of the land. In line with this, boys who are unable to pay bride price are encouraged to settle on their father-in-law's land and raise their families.

In the old days land and property could also be obtained through warfare. This in fact was the most common way of obtaining land. However boundaries were not static because the strength of each feuding party determined land areas. For example if clan A. was the stronger, it would push clan B. beyond the limits of its boundaries and set up new ones. Another day when clan B. was well equipped and strong it could regain some of its land back and keep on pushing until it set up a new boundary beyond its previous limits.

COMPENSATION PAYMENTS

The causes giving rise to the payment of compensation are many and varied. Compensation payments may arise due to such actions as damage to property (e.g. killing of pigs, burning houses, destroying gardens, etc.), use of someone else's property (e.g. land for gardening or setting up business ventures), fighting and killings, or verbal arguments leading to shaming and defamation, etc. Just as cases are many and varied, so are the types of compensation payments made to those affected. For example, you don't build a house for the relatives of someone whom you have just killed. Instead you make a big feast with as many as 20-30 pigs and present this to those who have been affected.

Compensation for Usage Rights:

Nowadays, compensation for the use of land is made in monetary terms, because most land that is being paid for through compensation is land on which people have begun business ventures like trade stores, service stations, garages or livestock industries. If one man has set up a business on another's land, and during the process wood and kunai from the land have been used, compensation should be paid.

Compensation for Damages:

Some people have settled on the banks of a river belonging to A. Since then they have fished from the river as well as used it for drinking and washing, thus depriving A. of the chance to use the river for his own good. As a result A. is demanding compensation equivalent to the amount used. In a case like this, it is only right that payment should be made as soon as possible, especially if someone else's property has been damaged through neglect, carelessness or through deliberate means. For example, somebody's house is burned due to a çareless person's ignorance. As a result, the person will be required to build a new house for those that have been affected. The trouble maker repays by building a new house and not making a feast or giving presents. Therefore compensation is made by replacing what has been damaged. However, nowadays, things are perceived in terms of money, therefore any judgement is based on money terms, hence the amount equivalent to the damage is arrived at and then compensation is paid.

Another example would be a case in which A. practices sorcery affecting B.'s garden, thus destroying his crops in the garden and therefore depriving him of the means of surviving. B. having found out about A.'s actions approaches a village elder and reports the incident to him. The elder informs A. to stop his practices, and to pay compensation for the damage. A. can do this in two ways. He can make a new garden for B., or can keep B. supplied with food until his new garden is ready.

Compensation in cases where fighting and killing are involved is a must in order to maintain a harmonious relationship between the people in the community. With regard to the former, a fairly common activity in the villages, both parties call their clansmen together and prepare an exchange feast to remedy the situation. This is followed by speeches from elders of both parties, and apologies are made. After this, normal relations can be continued. However, killing is an even more serious matter, and although it is a very rare thing, the first thing to do is "payback" for the killing. This may set off a chain reaction from the killing of a single man to many others. People are then drawn in and automatically take sides. The main preventive force behind such an action is consideration of the consequences involved and thoughts of what would happen to the community. Here again, huge feasts are made by both parties, and exchange followed by speeches by elders expressing their sorrow. However, nowadays with the introduction of money, as much as thirty or fourty thousand can be demanded. The existence of a whole community may depend on repayment.

HANDLING OF WEAPONS IN AN OFFENSIVE MANNER

The causes for the occurence of this kind of action are many: stealing, adultery, gossiping, etc. However, the seriousness of the case can only be determined by the person affected. For example, adultery is considered to be very serious, therefore husbands wouldn't give a second thought to the incident before challenging the other party to a fight. Compared to this, cutting a bunch of bananas is nothing but a minor problem which can be taken care of in other ways. However some cases, although considered minor, can spark off violent reactions which may take the form of brandishing dangerous weapons with the intention to kill. This may be so especially where one man considers another as his enemy and is always looking for the slightest reason to get at him.

FAMILY DISPUTES

Withholding wife from husband, that is, allowing the wife to live apart from her husband, is a move usually initiated by the girl's parents or family because they are not happy about certain aspects of the marriage, such as inability by the husband to pay bride price, the husband's incapacity to look after the family, unsatisfactory attitude of the husband towards the girl's family in regard to aiding in gardens, carrying wood, sharing food, etc., or mistreatment and abuse suffered by the wife from the husband. Parents withhold their daughter for an indefinite period of time, as a sort of punishment to the husband. Each of these situations will be discussed in turn.

Unpaid Bride Price:

The parents of a girl expect bride price to be paid when their daughter is wed. Therefore, with this in mind, the husband must prepare for the occasion so that the girl can be his rightful wife when they're married.

However if the husband is unprepared, some time can be set aside during which the husband can pay his bride price. If the husband is reluctant to meet the terms set, then the only alternative is to take the daughter back. The girl has some more freedom to visit or stay with her parents during this period of time because it is claimed that she has not been 'bought' yet.

Inability to Look After the Family:

This situation can arise when the husband is too lazy to find ways of keeping the family fed and clothed. As a result the girl is taken away from him for an indefinite period of time during which he should be able to place himself in a position where he can be more responsible for his family. During the period of time that this occurs, the situation will reflect a bad image of him and undermine his manhood and prestige in the eyes of the people.

Unsuitable Attitude Towards In-Laws:

A man's worth is also meansured by his attitudes towards the girl's family and more specifically, her parents. This means that he must help her parents in any way he can, and to respect and obey them as much as possible. This is for the sake of his own name as well as to please the girl's parents. Failure to observe this custom may lead to strained relationships between the two parties. This situation is usually climaxed by the separation of the wife from the husband, depriving him of the comfort and attention he usually receives from his wife. The solution usually is for the husband to remedy his attitude so that harmonious relationships can be continued.

Abuse and Mistreatment of Wives:

Once married, the husband is entitled to administer a fair bit of punishment to the wife but this should not become excessive, especially in the eyes of the girl's family, because as far as they are concerned, she is still part of their family. Excessive abuse and mistreatment can lead to fights, but most often the girl will be taken away for an indefinite period of time during which the husband is expected to cool down. After making sure that the husband is prepared to look after her and treat her well, the girl can be returned. In some cases the parents of the girl may demand compensation because of the disrespect shown to them. After the compensation is paid, the girl is free to join her husband.

Divorce:

The ultimate of all punishments to the husband is divorce, and as the term ultimate signifies, this is the last resort to which the woman can turn in the above situations. Particularly if bride price has not been paid, the woman is entitled to leave, and her family may support her. In fact they may coerce her to find a new husband who can fulfill the requirements expected of a husband. However, in a case where bride price has been paid, the husband's family is entitled to demand that bride price be paid back. Once this has been paid back, the woman is competely free to do whatever she likes.

In conclusion, I would like to point out that customary laws are not confined to the areas that I have talked about, but cover a very wide range of topics. What I have chosen to discuss are a few of the major problem areas in the villages. Although some of the cases seldom occur, they are important, like killing of a person. There is an unwritten law in everybody's mind which keeps a check on everyone's tempers: the knowledge of the social consequences of killings.

INDEX